T0194378

ADVICE FOR
MEN ABOUT
THE AMERICAN
WOMAN

TORIN REID

authorHOUSE®

AuthorHouse™
1663 Liberty Drive
Bloomington, IN 47403
www.authorhouse.com
Phone: 1 (800) 839-8640

© 2015 Torin Reid. All rights reserved.

No part of this book may be reproduced, stored in a retrieval system, or transmitted by any means without the written permission of the author.

Published by AuthorHouse   06/10/2016

ISBN: 978-1-4969-7301-6 (sc)
ISBN: 978-1-4969-7302-3 (e)

Library of Congress Control Number: 2015903448

Print information available on the last page.

Any people depicted in stock imagery provided by Thinkstock are models, and such images are being used for illustrative purposes only. Certain stock imagery © Thinkstock.

This book is printed on acid-free paper.

Because of the dynamic nature of the Internet, any web addresses or links contained in this book may have changed since publication and may no longer be valid. The views expressed in this work are solely those of the author and do not necessarily reflect the views of the publisher, and the publisher hereby disclaims any responsibility for them.

CONTENTS

INTRODUCTION

The very first thing that I want you to know is that I am a man. I am a man who has lived a significant portion of his life, a man who has seen and experienced the ups and downs in life. When I was younger, I saw life pretty much as I was raised, by two parents, in an intact family. The one piece of advice that I got from my mother about women was, if you take care of her, she will take care of you. The problem with that is that my mother grew up in the 1940's, and her advice was from that time. When it came time for me to have children, I did not think twice. Hey, you grow up, get married, and have children, have a family, and raise the children, like everyone else did. Sure, I had heard about nasty divorces and child support from others, and I dismissed all of that as that man's personal problem. I knew that I was not that kind of guy. I thought that I have always been pretty fair on the subjects of women and children, until one day I found myself standing in a hallway, looking at the painted cinderblock wall for the twenty-fifth time. I have been wondering, for a long time now, really, why am I here? A dozen other men are also in this hallway with me, lined up against the opposite wall, all on one side. We are all standing; there are no seats, at least not here. The occasional woman walks by, with an armload of files. She walks by, with her head down, so that she could avoid our stares. The air in here is heavy and still. Everyone is more or less silent. Just what is this place, you might ask? Jail? A bail bondsman's office? The DMV?

No. This is the third floor of the Queens, New York Family Court building on Parsons Boulevard in the Jamaica section of that borough back in 1995. The hallway is off of a main room where most of the people are awaiting hearings for a variety of life situations. Most of these life situations have gone bad – wayward children, abusive parents, abusive spouses.

But the hallway, apparently, is a special place for this group of men, who are not even permitted to sit. Every now and then, a court officer appears. His singular goal is harassment. He barks out "I said, stand up!" to those who have slouched, even though a couple of hours have passed.

I have confusion in my head, and all of the evidence that I could find, in my bag. There is about $13,500 in cancelled checks that I have made out to my son's mother. I had bought the baby's crib, and I was there to change the diapers. Later on, I paid for his karate classes, and bought toddler's outfits. I never hit my son's mother, nor even started a fight. There were no restraining orders; the police have never been called. So, why am I here?

Well, sooner or later, all of us who are standing here will have to go into a little room at the end of the hallway, because our children's mothers are all asking for something called child support.

I can anticipate your gut reaction. Child Support!! What the hell is this guy talking about? Really, is that what this guy is complaining about? Child support? You don't want to support your child? You're a deadbeat dad bastard!! You should be ashamed of yourself! You're not a father and you're not a man! You're a punk! Really, you were complaining about being made to stand? You should be whipped, tarred, hung, and whatever else they can think of!! This is unbelievable! You had to be forced to pay for your child? You're just a miserable bastard, who is trying to make your own child a bastard!

Well, I can understand all that. I have taken all of your scorn. I have heard all of these words, as well. They were either shouted at me or whispered behind my back. These words came from the faces of some family friends who don't speak anymore or from women who had laughed at me, or had been amazed ("Wow, she got that much!"). They were reacting to the overwhelming stereotype of the male deadbeat dad. People think that the family court is only for deadbeat dads. This is one of the biggest lies ever told, in history. In the United States, about 33% of all men with children (you don't have to be a biological father) end up charged with paying child support. Of that 33% of men who have been through the court system, 73% of that group pay the child support. When it comes to women who are charged with paying child support (it happens), 47% of them don't pay it, even when the amounts are far less than what a man typically pays. So, when was that last time anyone talked about deadbeat moms?

Listen, I believe - still believe - that every child should be financially and emotionally supported, in a way that should directly benefit the child. But, an important part - the most important part, as far as the woman is concerned, of the American child support system is all about putting the power of the state directly behind the mother (note the cop, judge and the lawyer on the cover). It is all about using this power to reduce or eliminate the father's influence upon the children, or to even drive him out of the children's lives. This is a kind of "public service" for women who now scorn and hate the man that they had children with. The system is this way because the American woman wants it this way. The majority of American family law was written by the American woman.

The negative effects of the fathers' absence upon the children are, apparently, to be ignored, up until the moment that the child is to be arrested by the police. Unfortunately, neither society nor the other children who may be victims can ignore this problem. Every study or survey will tell you that children who are without their fathers do worse in school, are more likely to abuse drugs, have sex earlier, and turn to crime more often than children with two parents at home. But, compared to the effort put forth for the American woman to receive her child support money (and alimony), any real discussion about wayward children seems to be insignificant.

But the negative effects upon the children are, in my opinion, far more important than the American woman's desire to drive the man down into poverty and insignificance. But in this American society, it does not seem to matter, because we have the good 'ol deadbeat dad to blame. If the children grow up OK, the mother proclaims that "I was the mother and the father". If the child grows up wayward, then the mother says, "Well, the father left". That statement puts her in the clear. And the so-called deadbeat dad shuffles on, with society's slop bucket on his head.

This perception of men, women and children in American society is so strong and persuasive that most men, "deadbeat" or not, have learned to simply keep their mouths shut on this subject. But here, in this book, I am not going to keep my mouth shut (or my keyboard at rest) on this subject.

And so, dear reader, now you have a decision to make. You can be comfortable with your gut decisions that I wrote about a few paragraphs ago. You can put this book down, and be comfortable with your prejudgments.

Or, you can read further, (especially you, mister) and find out why this bastard has written this book (the nerve of this guy!). You can continue to read this book, and maybe, just maybe, become enlightened. If you are not married, you can possibly save yourself thousands of dollars and years of heartbreak. You can read further, and allow me, to illustrate with words, just what the American heterosexual male is up against. And this is not just about child support. It's about the entire body of domestic and family law that now works against, and even criminalizes, fatherhood and the American heterosexual male, over the last 20 or 30 years. Indeed, at nearly every point of interaction between the American female and male, from first date to final divorce, there is a law or statue that will help to corral the actions of, or even penalize, whatever a man might say or do.

Listen, I am not being overwrought and I am not being vindictive. (Well, maybe I am, just a little). But, the larger point is, I am trying to get you, mister, to see the other side – your side – of this subject. Yes, there is another side.

Let's start off with that volatile subject of child support. Here is something that you, dear reader, might not know. Child support, as defined by New

York State, is money <u>paid to the state</u> that is later paid to the mother. Child support can also be defined, within narrow limits, by money <u>paid directly to the mother.</u> Please note that <u>only</u> the money that is paid by the father in this fashion is counted by the state as child support. <u>Whatever the father does directly for the child does not count as child support.</u> So that crib, and karate class, clothing, and about $13, 200 of that $13.5k was meaningless in the eyes of the court. And, it does not matter how much you spent directly on the child. It could be new teeth, braces, or even an education, it means nothing to them. All of that is deemed as a "gift", and is immaterial to the court as far as child support is concerned. Funny how child support isn't really child support, huh? But everyone still calls it that because it keeps you, the American male stupid and ignorant. And you would have stayed that way if you have not read even this far. Most of those stories that you might have heard about in the news media about "deadbeat dads" are about those men who have not paid money to the state. Whether or not these "deadbeat dads" ever actually did anything for their children is never revealed. And let me say this again, because a lot of you men don't like to listen (or read). The actual truth is, any money spent by the father on supporting the child is not recognized by the family court in New York; that money is considered a "gift" and it is not considered as child support. And a ruling such as this exists in many other states. The goal of this type of ruling is to strip the father's economic power away from the family, and making fathers bad in general. (Remember those deadbeat dads). The power and presence of the father is diminished by this in the eyes of the children, who often don't understand why the father's attention and money are diverted. Such a ruling makes the mother more powerful now that she has the backing of the state behind her.

I found out all of this, open mouthed and incredulous, in that little hearing room at the end of the hall. Little did I realize that this was only the beginning. There is more on this within the child support chapter of this book. And, listen, mister, if this was just about child support, this book would only be about half its size.

A large part of this book will be about the attitudes – and the body of law that follows – that is prevalent with today's American woman, and the attitudes that are prevalent with today's American society. Again, it is these attitudes that, over time has given a slow birth to the present body of American domestic and family law. Although these laws vary from state to state, the common goal among feminist lawmakers has been to offer for the American woman a life where any choice they make, is, for them, the right choice. Unfortunately, the costs for these choices, whether emotional or financial, do not just disappear into the thin air.

These costs are dumped onto the backs of men, children, and society itself. If you have any doubt about what I am writing here, please read what I wrote about women and pregnancy in the "So, do you want to be the father?" essay, and I dare you to contest that.

Listen, mister (and I am talking to men here) this book is from a guy who has found out all of these things, the hard way. This book is from a guy who once thought, well, yeah, a woman was all about breasts and curves and if you treat them right, they will treat you right. Yeah, that was a long time ago. And you should share this book with your teenage sons. The younger one is, the more that one can benefit from this book.

The goal of this book is not to engender hate against the American woman. Nor is it the goal of this book to set you against the concept of woman's equality.

The goal of this book is to make you, mister, an enlightened man. The goal of this book is to make you much more aware of how American society has changed, and how women's equality has changed now to a kind of "over-equality". The goal of this book is to make you aware of how much the present American society boxes you, the man in, and frees the female at the same time, using the domestic, family, and divorce laws. And on this point, I need you, the man, to go out and research these laws for yourself in the state that you live in. I cannot include all the different laws from the 50 states in this book. If you are not married, <u>do this research before you get married!</u>

The goal of this book is to make you a smarter man. A man who has learned to tear his eyes away from the T & A and look at where her head is at. I want you to be a more discerning man, and I want you to look below her skirt and see where her bottom line is at. And, mister, you need to do this, in varying degrees, with just about every American woman that you meet, from the one night stand to your fiancé. This is why the first part of the title of the book is "Advice for Men….." I'm not going to spoon feed you this advice nicely, like a calm and tolerant doctor. I'm going to give it to you straight, no chaser, just as if we were in a bar. And as for the rest of the title "….about the American Woman" Well, you can get into this trouble with any American woman, even the nice ones. Those divorce and family laws do not differentiate between good and bad women; they are for any American woman.

Bottom line – if you are a American heterosexual male, you really need to read this book, no matter what your current status is, married or not. It is never too late to learn. Again, this book has the potential to save you thousands of dollars and years of heartbreak. Don't misplace this book and leave it behind the couch. By the time you remember where this book is at, your girlfriend or wife might have put you out of your domicile. You don't really want to be in the position of having to tell that new guy who replaced you to get up off of your old couch for a minute, do you?

Oh yes. Just one more thing. I found out, years later, exactly why I was brought to court. (Remember, it was not because of money). My oldest son's mother, along with her new husband, was invited by my mother to a family gathering. My oldest son's mother noticed my new girlfriend. She had assumed that my new girlfriend was pregnant. And, yes, that's why I was summoned to court.

Mister, you'd better keep reading.

Torin Reid,

September 20, 2014.

WOMEN ARE LIBERATED
– ARE MEN?

In my hours of ruminating and thinking and even writing about the crux of the problem between men and women in today's American society, I feel that, perhaps, I might have found the problem at the center of it all. Like an astronomer who feels that he has found the alpha star, or that planet that might shed new light on the universe. Well – maybe not so much.

I feel that most of the problems between men and women in the United States stem from the fact that women, alone, have been liberated – for a couple of generations now – while men have not been liberated. Now, since liberation is such a widely interpreted word, let me narrow the definitions a bit so that you'll have a better idea of what I'm talking about.

I am not talking about the classical old style women's liberation movement, when women were freed from the roles of housewife and cook and when it made news that a woman broke into a job formerly reserved for men. Most of that occurred in the 1970's and 1980's, although one still reads of women moving into new roles today. The liberation that I am talking about is the liberation of American women, via the current body of family and divorce law, from responsibility of all kinds, especially their responsibilities to children, and men. Yes, I said their responsibilities to men, and more directly, the male child. What I see is that life's responsibility, for women, has been replaced by choice. With the proper excuse or alibi, an American woman does not really have to do anything, and escape sanction for almost everything. A woman does not really have to raise her children – the state can be made to raise her children, for free. A woman can put her newborn on a table in a hospital and walk away. A married woman can have a baby by another man – and have the husband legally forced to take responsibility (at least in New York State). And who pays for this lack of responsibility? The child, first and foremost, for years of feeling "less than" his or her peers in society because their mother abandoned them. Men pay because they have been separated from their children, and are often turned into wallets. And the price paid by the taxpayers is often the smallest bite out of society.

And, now what about men? Men have not been liberated from anything. Indeed, a man "is not a man" unless he does some very specific things, such as earn a living, not so much for himself but for his children's mother and their children (in that order). He must not fight with his woman, but he must become violent on demand (to defend her honor). Failure to do either gets him the "you're not a man" epithet. A man is ranked, in society and by other men and women, by how much money he makes (or more accurately, how much he appears to make). And this must all be accomplished within the shrinking legal cage that gets smaller each time some divorce or family law passes the state legislature and comes into effect. And while a man is not usually tasked with raising children, well, he certainly has to pay for it. I have seen a bum hauled in off of the street, still stinking, sitting in court, and being charged with child support. Now, one can say (and most men will say this loudly) "Don't make it if you can't pay for it!" But how do you force a bum to pay for someone if he is not willing even to take care of himself? And why is nothing being said to the irresponsible woman who laid down with this man? (I forgot – she is female, and so she is relieved of responsibility). And, it does not stop there. Some mothers are "not responsible" when it comes to the male child. Indeed, some men have been held back by our "modern" mothers and society and they don't even know it. Think of all the young men who have been raised without a father and now in their teens and twenties, and don't know how to go out and make their way in society. They sit at home lazy while their ageing mothers still support them.

To me, all of this that is going on between the American man and woman today is something like a person trying to drive a car that has one front wheel that turns and another front wheel that only goes straight. You are not going very far in such a car, and if you drive it anyway, you'll get a lot of noise and skid marks.

If we, as an American society, are going to move forward in the 21st century, we need to recognize that the progress of women and men in the present society has been uneven at best and a growing fault line between the sexes at worst. However, women, as a group, and most men, don't see any problem at all. In fact, the only men, and a very few women, who see a problem are those who have run afoul of it through the divorce process and separation from their children.

This makes for a certain amount of ignorance, for most people. Most American men are happily clueless. What problem could there be, with her pretty face, her bulging chest, her waspish waist, and her long legs and short skirt? This is where I come in, gentlemen. With this book, I hope to get you to finally look beyond the skirt, and all that could go wrong. Let me draw this analogy. In modern life, you have to buy insurance if you have a car. Most people think it is crazy to go ahead and drive without insurance, because what if an accident happens? Well, then you, as a man, should think that you should know what happens when things go wrong, with that pretty girl who is now your wife. By the way, a man who gets married and has children, has about a 50% chance of getting divorced and about a 30% chance of paying child support. If you had those odds of having an accident in mind when you got into your car, well, you would be a far more careful driver, wouldn't you? Maybe you would not drive at all.

The shame of it all is that when women and men allow themselves to "return to nature" – I'm defining this as doing what comes naturally in the absence of hate and pre – judgment – they find that they need each other. Ask any single mother who wants to close the bedroom door on her kids for a few minutes of peace; or ask any single man who is hoisting yet another beer in the bar, listening to the endless drone of the sports newscasters. That does not mean you can't live alone successfully; most people do. But, the nature of the human being is that we are social animals. And in a better world than there is now, we should not be afraid of living together and nor should we be afraid of sanction once we do separate.

Sometimes, a minority of those who are single end up trying to beat nature with some poor substitutes for a spouse, such as men who hoard material things, and females who hoard animals, and the like. And then there are those who just grin and bear it.

Yet, the grass may not be so green on the other side. For you married men, have you noticed that when a woman feels that you, the man, is making enough for the both of you, and she is comfortable within the relationship (according to her), all of a sudden, she wants to stop working, and become a stay at home wife? Yes, she wants to relax more, and let you shoulder all of the financial pressure. Some women just quit their jobs, and come home and announce that fact to their husbands. The funny thing is, most married men do not seem to mind. Perhaps it is because they are glad that their wives are no longer "out there", among the other male wolves, and, yes, she can be a better mother to the children. It is funny how many of today's liberated women yearn for the lifestyle of the 1960's. It amazes me how being a stay at home wife, even after holding a job, is so attractive to them. Hell, even Gloria Steinem got married. But still, in a retro way, this arrangement is still "natural" – if you and your wife can make the financial adjustment. And so, my question to you, the male, unmarried reader, is should you go out and get married?

I don't think so.

Why? Because the current society has mostly freed the American woman from responsibility to the child and her man. It's actually one thing to enter into a relationship with a liberated woman. There might actually be advantages to life with such a woman; but this depends upon both of your individual personalities. The real problem lies within the entrenched body of domestic and family law that backs up the current position of the American female, whether she is liberated within her mind, or not. (And she can always change her mind). Again, within this body of law, the American woman is almost totally liberated from responsibility to men and children. And you, as the man, will have to trust me and do your research and find out your states' laws for yourself. I can't pack the laws for all 50 states in this book, but I can give an example. For example, the divorce courts in five states – they are New Hampshire, Virginia, Michigan, Oregon, and Washington State all have the possibility of handing down a <u>lifetime</u> alimony judgment. Yes, she can have lifetime alimony. And, I'm going to repeat that all over this book, because you guys never get it the first time. How fine does that woman look now?

Think about this – does that sound anywhere near fair? Is it natural to get married with a law like that over your head? In California, the divorce courts there will call any marriage over ten years a "long term" marriage, and will reserve judgment over the divorce for life. Here also exists the possibility of a lifetime alimony payout. With the help of the state, she is basically entitled to pimp you out for her lifetime. To hell with that - I'd rather be a hoarder.

And it is not just those six states that I mentioned. The entire body of family and domestic law within the US is not static, it moves slowly along, tightening its sanctions against the man. With this in mind, is marriage still the "natural" thing to do? I don't think so. Not only that, but, should you get a divorce, you become responsible for that period of time that she decided to be a stay at home wife. Yes, that relaxed motherhood that she craves is, in court, pretty much chargeable to you, the man, in the form of "maintenance", or alimony. The divorce court in every state will worry about how much money she lost while staying at home, and her lifestyle, which must be upheld, at your expense. In New York, the divorced man is virtually guaranteed to pay out most of his salary in child support and alimony. Some New Yorkers have been ordered to pay more than they actually earn. When I show you, through this book, what can happen when a marriage or even a relationship with a child goes south, with the potential of being enslaved by the Venus flytrap of current marital law, it's a wonder why any man would still want to get married in the United States any more.

Listen, guys, I'm just trying to get you off of that mental first base. The American woman is behind you, because she has already circled the bases and has made it home – for herself.

Go ahead, man up, and keep reading.

SO, DO YOU WANT TO BE THE BOYFRIEND?

So, Do You Want To Be The Boyfriend?

In this book, we will discuss first things first. In this chapter, I am not going to tell you how to get a woman to be your girlfriend. I am not going to tell you how to be a better boyfriend to that woman. (There are many other publications for that purpose). Besides, life has informed me that, apparently, I don't have an earthly clue about those things. I am one of those guys for whom a night out is a total roll of the dice. What I want to do here is to lay out some ideas that might help you to work on you, for you. I want you to spend more time thinking about her – and not about her sex, or her toothy blowjob. I want you to think more about her as a woman. I want you to think more about her as a person. What I am saying is that I want you, the male, to become a smarter boyfriend, sooner. Don't take the long way around by letting them lead the relationship, and you, by the nose. Find out what is going on in their minds, as soon as you can. Now, you might ask, why "as soon as you can?"

Well, when you first meet a woman, what happens is (usually) this. You introduce yourself to her, and you converse with her, and, during that conversation, you try and make yourself as attractive to her as you possibly can to her. At or near the end of this first encounter, she will decide upon several possibilities – from giving up her phone number to giving up her body to you. But, let's face it, women choose us, and they choose at what level that interaction will be. Normally, we don't choose them. We, as men, may choose which woman to talk to. A man might make the first move, or even be invited to make the first move, but in the end, she has the final choice. Sometimes, women need to be reminded of this when they are bitching and moaning about the man that they invited into their lives. Women never seem to admit this. Since the choice of a partner is theirs, the smart man will try and find out why she selected him. Often, the choice she made may be superficial (he looks nice, he talks nice), but sometimes, the choice may be calculating (money, or a child and money). There are a million different reasons why a woman will go out with, and maybe sleep with a man; and a million different reasons why they won't. The goal here is to separate out the calculating women. Now, the calculating women are, of course, not going to tell you what their plans are, but, perhaps once the two of you get comfortable with each other, you can learn as much as you can about her. You may be able to read between the lines of the story that she has rehearsed for you. (One big red flag is if she, in her story, is always the victim, over and over). Talk with her friends if you can. One of her friends might be sympathetic to you, and "drop the bomb", or at least say something that may cause you to pause and think about it. Most women put out hints that are very slight, and a man might not be able to pick up that hint, because he is trying to look down under her halter top, or whatever. You, as the man, must rip your eyes away from her body, and look at her face. Look at her lips and see what is coming from there.

If you don't pay attention, you are not really going to get ahead of her, on this subject. And, keep in mind that she is doing the same thing about you. Not only is she gathering info about you, she is sharing this information with her girlfriends, or her mother, or both. In effect, you, the man, are now faced with what is basically a committee. You might be having sex with one woman, but you might be dealing with the opinions of five women. Indeed, your woman will discuss with her friends nearly everything that she has noticed about you. And at some point, the opinion of the alpha or most influential woman will matter to her more than your actions. This is why some women will give you their phone numbers but subsequently will not take your calls.

Think of it this way – just like how a group of men will get together and discuss this or that basketball, baseball or football player, a similar group of women have gotten together to discuss you.

But, while all that is happening on her end, you can continue to do research by yourself, on your end. Your male friends may not be able (or even care, beyond how the sex went) enough to offer advice about your girlfriend, but you can still work on your own. Don't grill her, of course, but converse with her. Get her to relax, and let her talk. Let me throw out one thing to consider before I continue. If she had sex with you on the first night that you met her, don't dismiss her as being "easy". She may have been "easy" with you because she really does like you. She may have been "easy" with you because she wanted to beat out a rival female who also had designs upon you. She also may have been "easy" because she likes sex. This is not a reason to denigrate or talk about her. It is hypocritical for a man to want sex all of the time and then talk about the woman who finally gave him some.

Other than that, when you are with her, take some time and let her talk. Women often talk about nothing – for hours at a time. Before the talk about those pumps on sale at Macy's versus those at Bloomingdale's forces your eyelids to close, try and steer the subject towards something you need to hear. Things like, how did she grow up? Did she grow up in a two parent household, or with just her mother? How did she leave her parents' home? Throughout this book, I will be asking the same, or similar questions over and over, and in more detail. I cannot stress enough that you, the man, need to know these things. Why? Because when it comes to marriage, you will be responsible for the relationship no matter who is actually at fault. You will pay for the divorce, if there is one. I will point out exactly how in later chapters. This is not being nosey; this is about protecting yourself.

Generally, what I am getting at here is how does she relate with men in general and you in particular? How did she fare in previous relationships? And how comfortable are you with her? Would you still be comfortable with her if her past included bouts of domestic violence? (And please read the chapter on domestic violence. It might alter your knee-jerk reaction on this subject).

Some of you guys might reason, well, I don't want to go through all of that; she's just my girlfriend. I can understand that. The thing is, that over time, any feelings you might have for her may deepen, and you might begin to overlook, or make excuses for, the things she does that would otherwise cause concern. Should the eventual marriage fail, guess who will be on the hook? You, the man. Yes, I am serious about this. You, mister, will be legally bound to preserve her lifestyle at the expense of your own. Most states index the length of alimony payments with how many years that you have been married. In five states, this alimony could last the rest of your life. Do I have your attention now?

This is why all this preaching is important. The more information that you have about her, the better a decision you can make about her. Is she the kind of woman with whom you can simply have sex, or is she a woman with whom you can share a life with? Or, what level in between? And, how would you compare this present girlfriend if another woman shows up in your life?

The goal for you, the man, should be is that you, not her, should make the important decisions about the relationship. Because, as you will see in subsequent chapters, you will bear the responsibility – and the burden – of this relationship, if something goes wrong.

USE A CONDOM!

This really should be a very short chapter, mister, so let me get right to the point. You should wear a condom, rubber, bag, or whatever you want to call it, during sex. There are no ifs, ands, or buts about this. Wear the damn condom. Should there be a why?

Listen, I'll be the first one to tell you that sex without a condom feels better, much better, than sex with a condom. I can wholeheartedly agree with you there. Yes, it feels good, and the orgasm feels better, when you come naturally (some call it "raw") into her. And maybe she'll never tell you, but chances are, that she loves it when you come deep into her. Privately speaking, most women love the feel of a man's sperm up in their bodies. They love it when they feel the man ejaculate up in them. Often, this triggers a woman's own orgasms. And usually, your sperm up in their bodies makes them think about you in a positive manner, long after you are gone. Gentlemen (and ladies), this is not nasty. This is actually nature. This is actually how men and women are supposed to be. But since nature has long ago been replaced by human nature, this is <u>not</u> what you are going to do.

There are some men that cannot really perform with a condom on. And, wearing the condom might be a problem for some of you older men. Some older men cannot achieve an orgasm while wearing a condom, as well. A solution to 90% of this problem is not so much the little blue pill as is the need for you guys to take better care of yourselves, and masturbate less. I'm not being flip about this, guys, I'm just laying this out to you. Your author is no spring chicken either. And like I stated above, I do understand "natural" sex. But I have learned also to understand what today's society is about. Today, we have human nature, which requires different responses. Today, we have today's sexual reality.

The number one reason for wearing a condom is to help prevent the transmission of sexually transmitted diseases. A sexually transmitted is a disgusting and nasty thing to have to deal with. A sexually transmitted disease has the potential to maim or kill you. Nothing ruins a relationship faster than an STD. Nothing is worse than one partner having to reveal to another that "I have an STD, and I gave it to you". Yet, morally speaking, there is no other way around this. You have got to tell her, or she must tell you, so that both of you can get to a doctor and get treated. And by the way, if she acts funny, and does not want to have sex, don't force it to happen. Her rejection just might be a huge red flag that she might have an STD. Again, morally speaking (there should be a little morality left these days) she must tell you. Or you tell her. Never mind the relationship; this is your fellow human being. Women have successfully sued men in court for giving them an STD. That's not to say that women cannot give out diseases; I just have not heard about any successful lawsuits of this kind from men. Why would you even want to run the risk, and be in this position? Now, I'm not going to go into all of the different kinds of STD's. That info can be had from other books, and that does not really matter at this point (before sex occurs). Be safe, and wear the condom.

The number two reason for wearing a condom is to prevent an unwanted pregnancy. You, mister, need to understand, that every time you plant yourself between some woman's thighs, as God intended, it becomes possible that a baby will come out, nine months later. Every time. I said, every time. I don't want to hear about how she's ovulating, or menstruating, or using the rhythm method, or whatever. Why? Because, women lie. Yes, women lie, especially about this subject. A woman may decide to have a baby with you, whether you want to, or not. A lot of them have the attitude of, well, if I have his sperm, I can do what I want with it, no matter what he thinks or feels. The decision to get pregnant (or, more likely the decision to have unprotected sex, and let's see what else happens) is a decision that she will usually make without you. The decision to get pregnant before might even have been made before she slept with you. It's her body, she reasons, she can do what she wants with it.

That decision to get pregnant, or allowing a surprise pregnancy to proceed, is a decision that was most likely arrived at by that woman and her friends. Your only "input" into the matter was from that drunken quickie in the parking lot about a month ago. You might have already forgotten about this. That sperm you donated will now potentially cost you hundreds of thousands of dollars, or more, over the next 18 years. In five states, New York included, that's twenty-one years. And there will be more on this in later essays, because you guys will forget or you because you are hard headed.

And, guys, I'm not finished yet. There is reason number three, and it is related to the reason above. It is called "peace of mind". Whatever sex might mean to a woman, I am never sure. What sex means to a man is that it is fun, and sometimes it is done for the sport of it, and it should not be a source of worry. Sex with a condom slows you down, and allows you to concentrate on her body and her mind. If she is dependent upon your orgasm so that she can have hers, just tell her that you are about to come. Whisper this in her ear, and don't shout it out like a fool. Sex with a condom allows you to move on to another day, and perhaps another willing participant. Sex with a condom ensures that there will be no babies, no hurried DNA tests, no appearances on the Maury show, and no trips to the family court. Compare all that to the ten second come that you might get "riding bareback". I think that peace of mind should triumph over those ten seconds. In fact, I know this. Trust me, these words of advice are coming from someone who wishes he had followed his own advice!

Is She Worth it?

Now, let's take this from the top, at least from a man's point of view, As far as women are concerned, at the top, or near the top of most men's thoughts is the subject of sex. As men, we see, and ogle women every day of our lives, from puberty until death. I understand that; I am right there, along with you. And, of course, with all that ogling comes the desire to have sex. Sometimes, the seduction or the conquest plays a role as well. Most men view sex as something that should be done for fun, and without reservation, and even for the sport of it. And I agree with all of that. After all, there is something to be said about pounding oneself into that wet, willing and warm place on her body. It's a pity that the male orgasm lasts for only about 10 seconds. Yet, to get that 10 second orgasm, some of us will move hell and high water to get to that woman who will provide us with that orgasm. And, if we can't get that orgasm, we will settle for the sight and sometimes the feel of a woman, usually in an overpriced strip club.

For all that is worth, gentlemen – I say, stop! Stop it right now. You might think, how dare I even write that, after all that buildup?

Because, generally speaking, in the long run, it isn't worth it. And, after some thought, I bet that most of you will agree with me on this. Of course, only you, mister, can decide what is "worth it". I know that. But I would like you to take a minute, and think <u>before</u> you go to the bar, or strip club, or whatever. And when you are there, take a second thought about your actions when you are in these places. Do you think it will be worth it when you look at your prospective lover in her face, and you do not understand the look in her eyes? Will it be worth it, when you realize that on the morning (or afternoon) after that night in the strip club, you find that your wallet is empty and you can't remember why? Will it be worth it, when you realize that this woman that you met at the bar or strip club, has been trying to rip you off?

Now, while I am in this mode, I have to give a shout out to any college kid who just might happen to be reading this, and all you other males as well. Do not take advantage of a drunken woman or a woman that is high, no matter where you met her. If she cannot talk, don't talk to her. If she cannot walk, don't walk her anywhere. Leave that task up to her female friends. You don't want to be seen as being the last person with her before she wakes up the next morning and tells the police that she has been raped. If you walk her anywhere, even back to the dorm room, she can say that she was kidnapped. Even if she has had multiple sex partners just before you walked up, if she says anything except "okay", (yes, that happens) do not do anything with her, and don't touch her (DNA). I'm serious about this. Your first task at school is to learn whatever your there to learn, not get involved in any long drawn out mess, what with all the women's talk about a "rape culture" on campus, and elsewhere. See the "For the Male college student" essay later in this book.

Again, most men like to have sex because it is fun and they like it. But most men, especially young men, have to learn to control and vent their desires in the proper manner. And this is becoming more and more important as the American woman seeks, through ever more restrictive laws and public shaming (witness the 2014 football player's domestic violence scandals). Guys, I personally feel that it is better spend less time trying to get with a particular woman, and to spend more time hitting on different women. Of course, go for the woman who gives you the best reaction.

As far as women are concerned, well, I could not possibly tell you for what reasons why a woman would decide to share her body. It seems to me that they follow their emotions and then justify it later. There are some women who want to have sex for the fun of it, at least at a particular time. There are not a whole lot of these women. Most of the time, these libidinous women are often called whores, by both men and women, but for different reasons. For men it seems that a woman is a whore when she has slept with others, but not him, or that he is surprised that she has had other partners. Mister, do not call a woman a whore when you feel that she was "easy". This is being hypocritical. Of all the things in life, you want sex to be easy, right? You, mister, should sit that "easy" girl down and talk with her. Maybe she likes you and thought that sex was the only way to get you. Maybe she sees something in you that you do not see in yourself. For you, this woman should no longer be "easy". She should be called "valuable!" Now, for women – they will call another woman a whore when she feels that this new woman was not selective enough, or when this new woman has slept with her partner.

Moving on now, it seems to me that most men are willing to accept almost anybody as a girlfriend. Indeed, a "girlfriend" could be someone who has had sex with a man twice, and is still hanging around. Most men don't mind this, and hey, it might even be OK, if both of you are just having sex. Listen guys, I am not talking about the "easy" girl here. By now, (the second time you both has had sex) you should have talked to her in order to determine what her motives are. I am trying to make you aware of the woman with a plan that she may not tell you about, such as getting pregnant, (are you using a condom?) or trying to make a murderous boyfriend jealous (!). After all, it is rare for a woman in any type of relationship to just keep on having sex, with no questions asked. Keep in mind that an American woman is more likely to have sex with some kind of ulterior motive in mind, even if it's just to influence you. The American woman seems to have been raised with a disdain for sex as fun, because it was drilled into her head that this was the place of the whore. Or maybe they have learned not to talk about it, at least with men.

But, more importantly to you, mister, is that the woman who is having sex with you may not be the woman who is good for you. She might want to give out a sexually transmitted disease (are you using a condom?) because, in her mind, all men are wrong for this, not just the guy who gave it to her. Or, she might be married, which might be OK, until her husband finds out. (and that outcome will be similar to the murderous boyfriend above). We, as men, are locked into the visual. We don't know anything else about her until she wiggled herself into our lives. And all we know is that we are glad to have her. We love her large breasts, the waspish waist, the perfectly rounded behind, and we are reduced to..... yes, ogling, and sometimes, drooling. The fact that she could be a serial killer never enters out minds until we see the glint of the bedroom nightlight off of her huge....knife, as she talks about her feelings, and expects us to agree because you, mister, are tied down. Or, she could be just a mental destroyer of men.

Guys, what I am trying to get at is, this. If you plan to do anything with her that is more than a one night stand (are you using a condom?) you need to know as much as possible about her, as soon as possible. It would behoove you to try and "read" her, or determine whatever you can about her, either with or without her conversation. A woman with a nice body should have a personality to match; and you, as the man, should be looking for the nice personality as well. Indeed, a woman's personality should be even more attractive than her body is.

Some of you guys have girlfriends who, in reality, are no good for you, and you know it as well. Perhaps you don't want to cut off your access to sex. I can understand that. Perhaps you just don't want to be bothered with going "out there" and trying to meet another woman, so you overlook her faults, again and again. I can understand that. But, you need to know that in a relationship like this, all she is going to do is get worse, because she knows that you are putting up with her bullshit. At some point, you are going to have to decide whether she is worth it.

Generally speaking, it would help most men (I'm not talking about the "playas" here) would spend more time trying to engage more women. The goal here would be not to build one's own private harem, but to find someone who might be closer aligned to you. This new woman, if you can find her, might be a better fit, rather than the woman that you met by "accident". Actually going out and doing this might not be that easy, because you will get "shot down" more often. But it is better to see what else is out there at the beginning of the relationship that to have wished that you have done so while stuck in the middle of one. And, have you noticed that women, even married ones, never really stop looking?

Perhaps you are not sure, either way, about your girlfriend. In this case, you should attempt to make things easier for yourself. When you are alone, simply take out a piece of paper, and list her flaws and attributes. Decide what, for you, would be a deal breaker. Decide whether you should keep her, or keep her until you find someone else, or whether you should leave that relationship.

Something else to do?

This is just another small musing of mine. I'm sure that many of you are probably aware of this, but there are a few of you who may not be aware, or who just didn't give it any thought. But, by mentioning it here, I would like to bring this subject up to its proper state of relevance among all men.

And, this is it. Have something else to do with your spare time, and your life, other than worrying about women. You should have, or get, a hobby or a pastime or something that occupies your time in a positive manner. The reason for having something else to do is so that you can have a mental "counterweight" to that not so successful pub crawl last night. Certainly, I am not saying that every night out will be unsuccessful or negative. But, if it is, or was, you will have something to get into that will put space, time and perspective between you, and that night out. Those of you who have a hobby or a pastime already know this. And, by the way, for those of you with something to do, you should not reduce the time that you spend on your pastime for her, unless things advance to the "being exclusive" stage.

Depending on what you do with your spare time, your hobby or pastime just might be a great way to find yourself a like-minded female. There is nothing better than having a friend with whom you can share your interests AND your body. Such a relationship, in and of itself can become wonderful and long lasting, if that is what you want.

Alas, there are a lot of women who just do not see things this way. A life together must be all about her, with little or no thought to how you wish to enjoy yourself. Some women see the time you spend on yourself as some type of necessary evil, like letting the dog out for a while, so that the dog does not soil the inside of the house. While you are gone, they will complain to their friends on the phone how selfish you are. Do not get into a long term relationship with these women.

That thing called Love

I thought about putting this in the next chapter (Do you want to get married?) but, the sooner you read this one, the better. And, I will repeat some of the same subject matter, in different ways, throughout this book. Why? Because, you guys are hard headed, that's why. (And I know that I have been repeating that) Plus, you guys think, well, if it does not happen to you personally, then it does not happen. This type of thinking is true, even with the good things, like with what I am about to discuss in the following paragraphs. What I am repeating here is how you, by making the right choice, can avoid a world of heartache and heartbreak.....and emotional poverty.

It is imperative that you know, in your heart and mind, when you are in a relationship with the right woman. You know it when you "feel" it. You know when you automatically consider her thoughts, or what she likes or does not like, in your next decisions. And, you know that she feels the same way about you. I'm talking about a woman who looks forward to growing old with you, rather than complaining about how much time has passed within the relationship. I'm talking about a woman who is willing to help run that relationship, rather than just coming along for the ride. I'm talking about the woman who asks "what can we do to make it better" rather than "what have you done for me lately?"

All of this is necessary because, if you do not look for these qualities, and your relationship fails, well, legally, most, if not all of it - is your fault.

But, before that happens, or before you get stuck in a dead end relationship, let's think a little about the "right" woman. In addition to the above, here is one more thing to consider. And the following is true, for both men and women. No matter how many people you meet in life, you are only going to have, at most, three or four true love affairs in your entire lifetime. Look, I'm talking about serious love, where she looks at your face, and you look at hers, for a solid minute or more. I'm talking about true love. I'm talking about that I-will –do-anything-for-you kind of love. I'm talking about love that will last a lifetime. It is from this vantage point, fellas, where you should start if you are looking for a serious relationship.

Make no mistake about it, if you wish to be serious with someone who is marriage material, start with the emotional top shelf. It would probably be worth it to go back and try and find someone with whom you might have experienced true love. She might be someone from high school, or college, or even junior high school. She might have been someone that you thought was too suffocating or clingy. She might have been someone whom you've rejected in the past (or, you were caught cheating) and she was not right for you because you were a player. But, you're not a player anymore (seriously!); you now want to settle down, now or in the future, and have a family. It would be a good idea to approach one of these women from the past, and invite them out for a cup of coffee. In the beginning, it should be nothing more than that. You are not going to destroy another relationship. But, you can find out what is on their minds, and see what she might say. Find out if she still might feel the same way about you, or if she has actually moved on. And, you need to do some thinking as well. Think about her – can you live with her, long into the future? Is the thought of this a little exciting? It should be.

If you are lucky – and, I mean real lucky – you might rediscover true love, with someone who is willing to make it last a lifetime.

Now, of course it is quite possible to find true love with a complete stranger. But you, the man, have to be careful here because women often fall in love with what you can do for them, and not fall in love with you. There's a difference.

Finally, one other idea would be to discuss your relationship situation with a trusted friend or relative who knows about love. Sometimes, they may be able to see things about you that you have not seen yourself. They might have thought about things that you might have missed, especially when you were in a relationship with a woman who has loved you. Or they might have advice about the relationship that you are in now. A small change for the better might make all the difference in the world.

And Other Relationships

Well, maybe not everybody can enjoy true love. It may be that you have missed your chance for true love, or that it just has not happened for you. The thing is, if you want to get into a long lasting relationship, and there are few other choices as beneficial as a long term relationship for men – it would be best to start from a position of true love.

If this is not possible, there is, I believe, what might be called a "lower level" of love, namely, a love born of convenience. Often, these types of relationships can last, as well. For the man, the chosen spouse is not the number one choice, or even the number five choice. For the woman, you (the man) might not even be the number 10 choice. Maybe you are about the number 25 choice. Each spouse, or more often, one spouse, makes a simple decision to be with the other person because he provides a good income or she provides good sex, and is loyal as well. These two people come to a decision to form a union. Guys, this happens more often than you think, and you might not even be aware that you are in such a union. If you were to ask your girlfriend whether this was true, chances are that she won't tell you. You will have to do the detective work on your own. For example, how often do you see her friends? If you don't see them at all, then perhaps she is ashamed of you. The thing is, if she selected you for your income, what would happen if you lost your job, or if your business suffered a downturn? What happens when you get older, and you (or her) are no longer able to take care of yourselves? There are other ways in which these types of relationships can go off of the rails. Over time, the agreed-to relationship may change, so that one spouse enjoys it less, and the other spouse benefits more. Then the relationship simply becomes a symbiotic one in that it "works", but little more than that. Worse yet, the relationship could turn into a simple "host and parasite" kind of thing where one spouse gets no pleasure at all. Then, it is simply a matter of time before the host gets tired of being the host. And while that "matter of time" can take years, the day will come when someone has had enough.

That other spouse might say, well, I loved you before, but now, I am leaving you or I am shipping you off to a nursing home. Frankly, I believe that this is the level that most marriages operate at.

Think about the many "arraigned" marriages, which are common in many Eastern and Middle Eastern cultures. The families of the bride and groom negotiate a relationship for their respective son and daughter. Often, there is a payment, or a dowry, to be paid from one family to the other. Don't sneer or laugh about these relationships. Arraigned marriages are actually the most common type of marriage in the world. And, because both the man and the woman within these marriages think first about the family, and then themselves, these types of marriages can last a lifetime. Frankly, many of us stuck up Americans could benefit from an arranged marriage. We could benefit from the guidance of those who have our best interests at heart. And if our parents don't look out for us, who will?

And, while I've written here about different types of relationships that are other than true love, these types of relationships (except the arranged marriage) often exist with everyone around them knowing that it is that way, except for the boyfriend or husband. The point that I am making here is that do you, mister, see any parallels in the relationships that I have described, with your own? And, are you comfortable with that?

Why did she choose you?

Have you ever wondered, exactly why she choose you? I guess that you can just ask a woman straight out, and most of the time, you will get an honest answer. Or perhaps you will get what she thinks that you want to hear. After all, there are a lot of guys out there. It's just something to think about, every now and then, in between trying to maneuver her into bed once again. There may be a hundred reasons why she might want to be with you and a hundred reasons why she won't. And, all women are individuals.

Generally speaking, woman want to be made to feel secure, and they want to be supported emotionally, and, often financially. And that is true no matter how lofty her economic status might be. They always want the man to make more than she does. This man must also be reliable and trustworthy and at the same time, entertaining and never boring. Also, this same man must also be sexually well endowed and sexually adventurous. And, it's all roughly in that order. By the way, these are only the headline requirements for most women. If you, the man, can fulfill the entire list, well, then, I guess you have no reason to ask why she chooses you. For the rest of us, we can take some time and think about this.

Perhaps we can make a rough analogy to this by using a woman's love for clothing. Let's equate that perfect guy – in her eyes – with that little black dress that most women seem to have. But, right now, in a sense, that little black dress is missing. That perfect guy isn't there. She knows that she needs that little black dress/perfect guy. The right kind of guy/little black dress does everything for her. He/it will maximize her attributes, and hides her flaws, and compliments her all the way around. That ultimate boyfriend, as well as the dress, would be the accessory of her dreams, if only she can find it (!).

Unfortunately, in the places where she is looking, or shopping, that "little black dress guy" is not to be found. There are other types of clothing/men all around, but none will do quite like the one she cannot find. She could change the places that she visits, but in her mind, it's not her fault that she cannot find the right fit for her, either a man or a dress. There are other tight dresses/guys that will hug her body, but will show off that one flaw on her body that no one is looking at. There are loose ones that are comfortable, but they just hang on her body and don't make her feel good.

Your mission, sir, should you choose to accept it, is to find out exactly what type of clothing that you are to her. Perhaps you are mister blue jeans guy because you are comfortable to her? Or are you there temporarily until mister little black dress guy shows up? Who really knows what was behind that sultry "yes" she gave to you the first night that you met? Then again, of course, you could just ask……

SO, DO YOU WANT TO GET MARRIED?

So, do you want to get married?

I'm going to go a little hard at you guys on this one, because I want you to take the time and really, really think about this. So, do you want to get married? What do you think that getting married will do for you? Think about these questions when you have the time, and when you are alone. I'm asking these questions – and more – because I want to impress upon you, the male, that you will be legally responsible for this marriage, no matter what actually happens or who is at fault. I am not against the concept of marriage. Having a lifelong partner is actually a plus. But the concept of marriage, in its' present form, loaded down with guarantees for the woman and sanction for the man, makes it imperative that if you do decide to get married, that she had better be the right person for you. Not the other way around. Again, if your marriage goes sour, you most likely will be responsible for alimony and child support, if you have children. You might lose the use of your house or dwelling that you have worked many years to pay for. You may have to endure extreme emotional hardship and loss of your children. I know that a lot of you guys flat out don't believe me. Some of you might be incredulous. Some of you will say "she's not like that", or "She would not do that to me", or "She loves me too much". All of this may be true – right now. Who is to say that these statements will be the same five years, ten years, or even twenty years from now? You, mister, need to keep in mind that she has the right to change her mind completely about you, and the current divorce and family court laws will back her up. So, I'm going to ask you again, what does marriage mean to you – really? Is this whole thing like the old internet joke, that marrying her makes it illegal for her to be with someone else? Or are you just tired of hearing your girlfriend complaining and moaning that the two of you are not married? Is she complaining that the two of you have been boyfriend/girlfriend long enough, and now, you should "commit?" Does she say over and over that she has "invested" enough time, and now there should be results? Well, how about this – what does marriage mean to her? Is it all about her feeling secure – potentially, at your expense? You need to pose those questions to her. A woman once told me, with feeling, that a married woman "has rights", meaning, that she could rely upon the current draft of divorce and family laws that come into effect the second that you sign on the dotted line. After maybe three generations of women's liberation, along with the liberated woman's opinion of men, I find it incredulous that the overwhelming majority of women still want to get married. They prefer a man who makes enough money for the both of them to live on, so she can be a stay at home wife, just like her great grandmother did back in the nineteen fifties. For the third time, guys, you really need to think about this. And, yes, I touch on this subject, more or less, in many other essays within this book.

What if you are already married?

I wrote this essay for the guy who is already married, and is not presently considering divorce. Or, maybe, just maybe, those previously forbidden thoughts of divorce are entering into your mind. What should you do?

Well, the advice from me is to find a lawyer – a good divorce lawyer – on your own time, and by yourself. Why would you need a good divorce lawyer if you are happily married? Because, you would want to see where you are "exposed", that is, find out where the legal weaknesses are in your relationship, and what you are liable for. Did you sign a prenup? Did <u>she</u> sign a prenup? Would it be likely that you would lose the house? (Generally, yes, especially if there are children). What about alimony? (Depending on the state you live in, and how long you are married, you may be liable for lifetime alimony payments in several states -- seriously). Please see the other, related chapters, in this book. And why would you want to know all of this bad news? Because this way, you will have no surprises if that storm appears on your horizon. This way, you won't have to make decisions in an atmosphere of crisis. A good divorce lawyer can, with an hour's paid time, frame for you a snapshot of just what your life might look like, after a divorce. I can bet that no other writer of men's issues ever advised a man to do that. Most people in American society prefer that the American male, as a group, live in ignorance about the subject of divorce.

As the man, you may have to think about your marriage more and more as you would a business. You are doing yourself a disservice by not knowing your assets, almost to the penny, and your liabilities, almost to the penny. The thing is, in other facets of life, you have already done this, for example, when you sit down to buy insurance. You had to have had an idea about how much of your assets (usually, a house or car, and its contents) that you needed to "cover", or protect. You had an idea about how much you can pay, and to what degree, with a deductible, and so on. Try and think about the state of your marriage in the same way.

Now, after that good lawyer lays down to you what the possible liabilities of your marriage are, you should ask him what you can do to make those liabilities smaller, or maybe even disappear altogether. And, if you have time after that lawyer helps you to reduce your liabilities, ask him or her (preferably him) to show you some of those egregious and overreaching divorce laws in your state. Generally speaking, divorce laws are the worst on the coastal states, east and west, and those laws seem to be not as bad in the south and parts of the west. In this book, I can only show you some of the domestic and family laws of New York State; and some examples from other states as well. It would be impractical to feature laws in all 50 states in this book. But, gentleman, be advised, some of those laws are surely there, in <u>your</u> state. You should be more than ready to do your research. It might help to look at the divorce and family laws of a neighboring state, as the laws there might be "better" or most suitable than the ones where you presently live. Would it be possible to consider moving to that state? Try and float that idea first, with your lawyer, and, later, with your family. Of course, you are going to keep the reason why secret.

Go ahead, skip a couple of nights out, save your money, and pay your lawyer for an hour of his time.

If you are not willing to do this, you can also take the time, alone at first, to look at the state of your marriage. Often, men, in the act of chasing a paycheck, fall into a rut. Sometimes, this rut or work cycle can get so deep that the wife and children begin to feel neglected. Maybe it is time to take a weekend, or even a week's vacation, and spend it from sunrise to sunset with your family. This is important, even in this new age of lowered expectations, and lower salaries.

If you feel that this is the case, well, then, you should make the first move. Your wife and children should be looking to you for leadership. So make the first move and spend some quality time. Your efforts may be well rewarded.

Then again, the problem that you might sense within your relationship might go deeper than that. There might be some ill will or feelings that your wife may, or may not have shared with you. She might feel as if you were ignoring her for a long time. This is something that you will have to set aside a block of time and discuss this with her. Just sayin'.

Who is the person you are marrying?

Yes, who is the person that you are marrying? Who is she, really? I know that you know who you fiancé is. What I am asking you, do you know your fiancé, or wife to be, well enough for a 30 to 40 year relationship? Even more importantly, is she ready for a 30 to 40 year relationship? Does she really have what it takes to be married to one man, over the long haul? Or is getting married all about her feeling secure, at your potential expense?

Most marriages are, in fact about her feeling secure, and it is all about her being able to build her personal life on top of your money, mister. Even in these days of "full" women's liberation, most women prefer, at some point in their lives, to be married and secure. Indeed, the more wealth that you have, the more "old fashioned" they are liable to be. This is why, in this essay, we will discuss whether your girlfriend/fiancé/wife to be is really marriage material to begin with. I have touched on this subject in other essays, but in this chapter of the book, I now assume that you are serious about this. The questions that I am going to ask you to think about are, frankly, kind of obvious. But, maybe you may not have ever thought about these questions in this way, or from this new point of view. It is important to confront the hard truths in what you see about her. If you currently have no one, it is essential for you to have a defined, concrete ideal about the kind of woman that you would marry. Trust me, women definitely have their own ideals about the men that they would marry. So, again, let me pose a couple of the most important questions that you need to know, or at least ask, about your soon to be wife.

Question one: Were her parents married? Needless to say, this is very important. When your girlfriend was growing up, did she grow up with both of her parents? Did she see the everyday tasks of a marriage, good or bad? Either way, she might be better equipped to handle the ups and downs of a relationship better than a child of divorce. Your girlfriend, if she grew up as a child of divorce, might be more inclined to take the "easy" way out by getting divorced. It is up to you to find out how your girlfriend really feels about this. Don't accept the nice, sweet answer to that question that she wants you to hear. Listen to how she talks when she is with her friends or is talking about someone else's relationship. If she says something like "….I wouldn't accept that in my relationship, either he picks his clothes off the floor, or I would get up and leave…", well there you have a partial answer. Most women see marriage as something comfortable to them, and as soon as a marriage becomes uncomfortable to her, then she wants out. If your girlfriend is not true to you and does not really love you, your thoughts and feelings do not really matter to her. Obviously this is not the woman for you. It is up to you, mister, to find out just what lessons her parents, and especially, her mother, have given to her. Hopefully, you have met a woman who has a concrete idea of what efforts that a marriage demands, and is comfortable enough with you for the long haul. Hopefully, you have met a woman who saw her parents work together towards a common goal, and she would like to do the same thing with you. Hopefully, you have met a woman who can ride out the lows as well as she can enjoy the highs within a marriage. Now, if you can find a woman who can do all of that at least some of the time, well, then, mister you've got gold. Treat her like she is gold. Please read this and understand, mister, I'm trying to get through to you. Some guys go through their entire married lives oblivious to the fact that they should have taken an active role in choosing their wives. They just got married because of the pressure from their girlfriends ("We've done this long enough!"). Now, these men are obligated to spend the rest of their lives mentally working the 40 acres of their wives' fertile minds just to stay in place in their lives, forever dancing to the woman's manipulations. Some men are actually miserable living like this but they know that they will get hosed down in the event of a divorce.

If your woman grew up as a child in a single parent household, it may not necessarily mean that she is not fit for marriage. Maybe she has done some mental homework between those earlier times and the present. But, generally speaking, she is not as "top shelf" as the woman who has grown up within a two parent household. And what I mean by that is that she has no real experience with married life. She often has no idea of how to be married, beyond her desire to feel secure. On top of that, you, the male, might be the recipient of – maybe even the victim of – her feelings of abandonment, or even the mothers' feelings of abandonment about those long gone men in their lives. Her hidden attitude might be what her mother has said ("Get them before they get you!"). With such a woman, you might be forced to always deal with the ghosts of past men in her life.

For those women that have children, this could be another complication. How does she feel about the biological father? How do her children feel about their father? Do they even know him? If you had children with a woman who has not resolved these issues with her own children, well, it is possible that the child you have with her might not know you.

Question two: How did she grow up? This is NOT question one re-written. Here, I am asking you to take an even closer look at how your girlfriend came to be the woman that she is today. I know, some of you guys might see that as intrusive, but the real goal is for you to have the best possible wife so as to minimize the consequences of divorce and child support. Be a little (okay, maybe a lot) nosey, and find out how the rest of her childhood went. What else did she learn in her childhood? What about her siblings or her friends? Did she draw any life lessons from this time? In total, was her childhood functional, at least? Or, perhaps, did she watch her parents fight, more than a few times? Were these fights just family feuds, or were they life threatening? Were the police called once, or often? Indeed, what do the police mean to her? Are they a type of protective "Big brother" on call, for those times when "her pet" (meaning you) is out of control? Some women actually enjoy the part of having the last laugh while you, the man, is led off in handcuffs. Did she ever mention in a conversation, "Well, I put him in jail…..". Are you still there with her after hearing that?

The lesson for you, the man, to take from all this is to find out how she views all of those things that I mentioned. Find out how they affect her today. Women seem to hold on to negative or life changing events for a long time. This could potentially mean a lot when it comes to dealing with you. You, the man, should take some time to talk to your girlfriend about some of these things that may be in her past. Sit her down with a bottle of wine and converse with her. Don't grill her. Let her relate to you about what may have been the defining moments in her life. Then you must decide privately whether or not she has been able to heal, or move on from those incidents in her life. After that, you decide whether you will want to deal with her unsolved problems if she can't.

Question three: How was her sex life? Now, this is one aspect of her life that you will be the least likely to know, at least on a casual basis. Of course, it is not necessary to know about all of her previous sex partners. Actually, you really do not want to know about all of her previous sex partners. What I am getting at is, did she have more or less normal relationships while she was growing up? Did someone touch her when she was young? When did she lose her virginity? What are her views about sex? Is sex to her something to lust after and enjoy? Or is it more like a chore, like walking the dog, or feeding the male beast (meaning you). Perhaps she suffered some kind of rape or abuse that has led to a hidden, lifelong resentment of men? Or is it that she just does not really enjoy sex?

Often, a casual conversation about early relationships will reveal how she feels about the present. Again, the details are not important, rather, it's how she feels about those things today are important. How she feels today will say a lot about how she will deal with you in the future.

Sometimes, listening to her talk about her past just might reveal another side of her that you are not ready for. She might reveal that she has had a lot more sex than you, and that also affects her sexual life with you today. My question to you, mister, is can you handle that revelation? Most women prefer that you should be the more experienced person. This is one important thing that you should keep in mind, mister. Remember, we are talking about a lifetime commitment here. As with all the other facets of her life, you need to take some time alone, and see if you can live with all of this new knowledge about her.

Question Four: What is she willing to do for this marriage to you? If some of you were paying attention during the first three questions, you would have most of your answer to this question. And at the same time, some women don't even have an answer to that question. Most American women have a detailed fantasy of what she requires for a long term relationship. Some of these women give very little thought about your feelings within a marriage. All she cares to know that she is married and that she got rights. (See elsewhere in this book.) The American woman often feels that she is the prize of the relationship; all that she really has to do is get up in the morning and look good. That attitude is a really big red flag for any long term relationship. No matter how beautiful she is, sooner or later, you are going to get used to that beauty and then her personality will jump out right in front. The next man, seeing only her beauty, cannot understand why you treat her the way that you do, now that you see her for the person that she is.

Listen, if a woman cannot reel off what she is willing to do for a marriage – a marriage to you, the man – (and you need to hear something more specific than "make you happy") then she is not ready to be your wife, bottom line. She might be ready to get married, but it should not be to you, if you are smart.

Don't limit yourself to just these questions when it comes to your prospective wife. Remember, if there is a breakup, the law is squarely on her side. Therefore, it is up to you, the man, to be fully satisfied with the tangibles and intangibles within the answers that you get to the questions that you have asked her. And, last but not least, include your gut feelings in your decision. After all, you are going to be the responsible man in this marriage, one way or the other.

Ancient History - and the "Deal"

Here is something to contemplate, hopefully while you are at home, and not in the back of the limousine, on the way to that vaulted altar, deep within the church. I feel that I have to bring this question up. This question, which you – and her might have forgotten to discuss – maybe intentionally – but at some point you and her will end up talking about it. Perhaps it is one of the hidden and at times, distasteful aspects of modern marriage, but I will proceed to the question anyway. The question is, what role are you, the male, expected to fulfill in this relationship? What will be her role? Have you talked about this, or do the both of you have "expectations?"

Well, allow me to give to you some historical background on this vaunted institution of marriage, and what it used to be within society, and what it is, now. Let's go back, say, one hundred years. Back then, there were concrete expectations of both men and women in society. Men had their role in being the provider and role model for the male children. The woman kept the household up, and everyone fed, and was the role model for the female children. Sometimes, she worked as well. Somehow, this all seems quaint and old fashioned, as seen through the dim mists of time, right?

Wrong. Those roles in life, for men or women, were cast out of practicality, and not prejudgment. And most certainly, those roles were not cast because men were out to enslave women, as some feminists would have you believe. Those roles were, themselves, descended from an even earlier time when most people were farmers, and hunter-gatherers. It was almost always left up to the male to tend to the farmland, and also attempt to trap and shoot small animals for consumption. There were many exemptions, of course, but this was how most people lived. Nearly every day was a full workday for both the man and the woman. You either farmed or caught something, or you starved. You had to plan ahead for winter and any lean times that might befall you. You had to grow enough crops in order to feed yourself and your family, and maybe make a small profit from the sale of some of the crops. The woman had a full workday because doing some of the simple household tasks took much longer to perform than they do today. For example, washing clothing with a washboard at the creek took several hours compared with 40 minutes on today's washing machine. An animal that was caught for dinner had to be skinned and prepared for cooking, as compared to the wrapped meat from the supermarket. A couple had to depend upon each other, mostly sight unseen, in order to succeed and survive. There weren't any vacations back then.

Over time, people began to leave the farms and began to move into the cities and towns. Farming changed from a source of sustenance to a profit based business for the few that stayed. But the division of domestic work stayed the same because men still worked long hours at whatever jobs that they could find. Most men who were not lucky enough to have a skill or trade or who were not rich enough to become a business owner had to work those long hours to provide for their families. Less than one hundred years ago, Saturday was a workday just like Monday to Friday was. Sunday was truly a day of rest – it was not just a religious reference.

Society – and your wife - judged you, the man, on how well you were able to provide for your family. Things are almost exactly the same for you, the man, today. A woman was expected to get married and have children. Society judged her on how well she could do both of those things. Today there is little or no real judgment for the American woman, whatever she does. Yes, it may have been unfair back in the old, old days – as were a lot of other things that were considered "normal" - such as lynching, and smoking. But as far as the family unit was concerned, for the most part, things worked. Most families stayed together for the children, and because it was the right thing to do. Of course, back then, there were breakups, and divorces. Nothing was absolute, then as it is now. But men and women were encouraged – even harangued - to think about others before thinking about themselves. And when there was a breakup, it was often the children and the woman who suffered.

Within American society, life began to change, slowly, over time. The Saturday work day, now pared down to a half day of work, was finally eliminated after the close of World War Two. During the 1950's, there were many small inventions and gadgets that helped to save time with the domestic tasks at home. The advent of the television demanded more leisure time, since you had to sit down and look at it, as opposed to just hearing the radio. The civil rights movement began in earnest. In the late sixties, American youth began to confront the decisions of those in power by protesting the Vietnam war on a national scale. The women's movement, nascent since the early part of the 19th century, also began to make itself widely known. Still, the family unit held together. That "deal" where a man works and a woman keeps house, was still backed up by society, held together, even if the larger society was now less judgmental about this, at least towards women. You might have even known some of these people. They may have been your grandparents, or even your parents. Again, life was not perfect. Not everybody was happy, and not everyone stayed married. But most people did, and often for the sake of the children.

Today, of course, things are, on the face of it, radically different. The word "family" includes far more than a man, a woman, and a child. And while the man still must provide, or face judgment, nearly everything for the woman has now become a choice. Today's woman, within a relationship, generally does not have to cook. She does not have to clean. Today's woman does not have to do anything "for" you or the family. I am not saying that she won't do anything at all. I am saying that, legally speaking within today's domestic law, all of the above is simply a choice for her. Society no longer has little or no influence on what goes on inside the home. Religion can make a difference, but that depends on how religious you are and how religious she is.

And, there is something else to think about. Most American couples who are in the middle class or the working class might not even have that choice as to whether she stays home or not. There are many couples where both the husband and the wife have to work, to even survive. Most Americans have paid very little attention to the financial reversals of the entire middle class that has been going on since the 1980's and the sharp drops in buying power since the financial panic of 2008. Most younger Americans today may not even realize that their parents, who may have been stuck together in marriage but could afford a house, may actually enjoy a better financial life then they have had so far. Coming back home after college and living under the weight of huge student loans was unheard of back in the last century.

Think of all of this, and discuss all of this, the next time that you have some time alone with your girlfriend or fiancé. It is upon you, mister, to make sure that your girlfriend or fiancé is a real potential life partner. Getting the things in life such as a house or a car will cost more out of your pocket then it did your parents. Caring for a child will cost even more than that. Make sure that the both of you can face these realities together.

Married Life with the Wife

Hopefully, mister, you might have read this far without having committed yourself to marriage. If you are already married, then I am willing to bet that you will see at least some similarities in this essay to what you may have experienced within your own relationship. Or, you might know someone else who has. What makes me so sure of this? Well, it's mostly because of the many conversations that I have had – unprompted, mind you – with many married men over the years. These conversations have often started elsewhere but then turned towards life, and then to married life, and the wives within those married lives. Of course, I do not know about everyone's married life. But I know of more than a few. I know enough so that I can comment on this.

I might be a little unscientific here, but I would guess that perhaps half of all currently married men have so many problems with their marriages that if they had the chance to do it over, they would not get married again. Or at least, they would not get married to the same woman. More than a few men feel trapped within their marriage, being tied down with the wife and kids and the huge expense of breaking up. The core of the problem is that their wives did not turn out as expected. The girlfriends that these men have proposed to are not at all like the wives that they are presently married to. A lot of the problems have to do with money. That is discussed in more detail in the next essay.

Some men are disappointed because they realize too late now, that some women don't even know how to prosecute a long term relationship. Most American women want to get married, but these women are thinking about their own security, and nothing more. Most women see marriage as a 'what he is supposed to do for me' kind of thing. Many women are not even aware of what they are supposed to do for their man within a marriage. If you, mister, think that I am lying, just ask a woman what does she thinks that a man is supposed to do for her when she gets married. She will respond with a specific laundry list of items. She might nail you down for 10 or more minutes with her list of demands. Wait patiently for her to finish. Now ask her what she is willing to do for her husband. More than likely, she will respond with cloudy generalities. There might be three sentences' worth in her reply.

It needs to be said here that you, as the man, should have made it clear what your expectations were before marriage. Now, some of you guys must now take a retroactive look back through her pre marriage life, and only now do you see that she has never really known a stable relationship. There are a lot of women out like that, fellas. That's why I asked you in an earlier essay "Who is the person you are marrying?" This is why I have been haranguing you on this subject all through this book.

There is also the kind of woman who either depends upon, or lets their woman friends in on every major decision about your marriage. Her friends might have as much, or even more influence over her than you do. You might have last heard about these women when she told you that she was pregnant. Again, as you watch your wife's actions and reactions (and you should be watching) it is as if you might be dealing with five women, but you only have sexual access to one. You might not even have met this friend of hers who has so much power over your wife. Or, worse, this powerful "OZ" woman hidden behind the curtains might just turn out to be a man. Mister, let me tell you right now, either you put a stop to that or you get your own female confidant. A wife should not have any close male friends or work husbands that she invites vicariously into your lives. What this really means is that deep down, she does not trust you, and she wants to feel secure and be able to jump into another relationship should things go bad between you and her. A male friend or a work husband is often a "man in waiting", never mind that modern life bullshit.

Even worse, that unseen hand that is steering your marriage might turn out to be her mother. This possibility is even more likely to occur. Her mother might have learned to accept her spinsterhood after burning up her relationships only to turn her energies towards her daughter and influence your married life. It could take a very long time, and much detective work, to root out and confront this behavior. And when you do, you might find that your wife might not want to change her relationship with her mother because she values her more than she values you.

Then, there is the woman who considers herself to be very intelligent. Sometimes, she considers herself to be more intelligent than you. These women will often work to build for themselves an entire parallel life, in which you, the husband, might play a minor or insignificant role. The parallel life that these women build is often within their working lives. They may also have a "work husband" as in what I wrote above, only this time they will try and control the work husband as well. It often starts with getting the work husband to buy the shared lunches and then keeping him close. Close enough to keep the flirtation hot and the other female co-workers away but not so close that you, the husband at home, are able to "smell" him.

Sometimes, you might be able to get a clue as what may be going on at the workplace when you ask her how her day was. (Are you asking her?) If she names the fellow employees and tells you about her day in detail, then your position as a husband should be secure. If you get, as a reply, one sentence answers or even excuses, then perhaps it is time for some detective work. One big red flag is if you are never invited to a work related function. Some married women see the married life simply as an emotional bungee cord that they can stretch out from the married life at certain times and yet still feel secure. They do not see married life or the husband as the total sum of their lives.

Now, of course, if you are reading this by the fire and your wife is nearby and all is well and dinner is cooking, well, that's fine and dandy. But you need to know this anyway!

The Married Woman and Money

This subject is one of the main sources of anger and discomfort among married couples. Actually, money is one of the main sources of anger and discomfort among any two people who have agreed to spend time together, whether it may be in a casual relationship, roommates, or even a landlord and tenant. But here, we will focus upon the married woman, and what she is liable to do with money within the marriage. Let us look at the stay at home wife, and then the working wife, and what you might be able to do about it as the husband of one of those wives. The one thing that seems to be universal, whether or not the wives worked, is that a lot of women don't seem to care how much effort it takes for you, the husband, to bring that money home. What they do care about is how much money you bring home. Once they find out how much your weekly paycheck is, they will count on that same amount to come out of your pocket each week. Don't ever come home with less, or have a real good reason why you do have less this week. Life will change around the house if you do come home with less, and you don't have a good excuse. Indeed, if you really want to find out what kind of wife that you really have, take two weeks' vacation from your job and tell her that you've been laid off. You might be surprised – good or bad – with the reaction that she might have.

Women's advocates will often tell a stay at home wife or mother that the money that you earn is actually her money, and that she should spend it accordingly. I do not know whether you are comfortable with that. I certainly would not be. Most stay at home wives are likely to interpret that as "spend freely", and let you, the man worry about the financial pressures of the mortgage, bills, etc. Most stay at home wives do not need that incentive from the women's advocates. They spend a premium upon themselves and you will not know where all your money went. Furthermore, they will focus mostly upon the things that interest them and the children, if you have any. Many of these wives will pay little attention to whatever your interests are (except maybe for your birthday and Christmas holiday season) unless that interest is something that the both of you (or the family) does together. Otherwise, you might have to fight with her to just to get some of the money that you've just earned for what you want! It's amazing sometimes, just how badly that kid needs braces right now, or that microwave needs replacing right now, or that couch needs replacing right now!

A lot of these women spend your money roughly, in the following order. Her entitlements ("what I deserve"), her needs, then the children's needs, and finally the household needs. If you, the husband have any doubts about this, simply ask her what she did with her day. Have her detail, a little, about what went on. Now, you listen, don't just hear, how she has made up her day. Chances are, the hairdresser came before the baby's new blanket and the food shopping.

The husband of such as wife will have to take a proactive stance over the family finances. While it is impractical to oversee every penny, you will have to put your foot down and put her on a budget, with a set amount to spend each week. You must ensure that you are putting away a set amount each week as savings. You must watch the bills, even if she pays them, because some bills can get out of hand, like a cell phone bill, and she might neglect to tell you. Enforce cutbacks if you have to. Some women really are like children, when it comes to money, and you might have to treat them as such. Otherwise, she'll drive you bankrupt.

The working woman is not all that much different from the stay at home wife. But the working woman prefers to keep as much of the money that she earns to herself. This woman prefers that her money not be comingled with yours, or even be used for household expenses. Now I understand, that in many relationships, that the working wife has to commit the money that she earns towards the household. There might not be any room for money games or chicanery in such a household. But when there is room, chances are, there will be. There are many married, working women who will maintain bank accounts (usually, under their former last names) with money that you, the husband, are not supposed to know about. These women have been known to brag about this among their friends. I know this is true, because I heard them. There are many married women who will sit down with you and cry with you about how bad the bills are. They will vow to be better with you, and suggest to you on how to cut back, on your end, of course. They may even promise to cut back on their luxuries. What will really happen is that you will know longer hear about their luxuries because it is now being covered by that money you are not supposed to know about.

Alternatively, some woman will hide their pay stubs in the hope that you will become ignorant, over time, of exactly how much they make. Sometimes, during their workday, the working wife will spend an exorbitant amount of money every day upon herself. She will always tell herself that "she deserves it". She might enjoy an expensive lunch on her lunch hour, or she might shop for some expensive shoes or clothing that she will sneak into the home later on. While it can be said that everyone might "deserve it", there comes a point in time where the thrill of deserving it over and over goes from being something special down to something normal. Now, she needs it to "maintain", and, lo and behold, this is now an addiction. And now this addiction is taking money away from the family, and putting yet more financial pressure upon you, the male. Very few women see it that way, but I just told you the truth. I once worked with a woman who ate lunch every day at a fairly expensive restaurant, while promising her husband that she would lose weight and save money. The thing is, why promise someone anything if you are not going to make good on it?

Again, you, as the husband, need to be proactive in cases like this. Find out, anyway you can, exactly how much money she makes. You need to sit her down, confront the problem, and work out a budget. Then, the both of you should put your actual, base salaries together, and then you apportion a percentage of each person's salary towards the household bills. For example, if you make $62,000 a year, and she makes $38,000 a year, that's $100,000 total income. Now, add up all of the household bills on a yearly basis (and, that better not exceed, say, $65,000, or the both of you are in trouble!). Of the total amount of the household bills, you should pay 62% and she pays 38%. This amount should be direct deposited, from both of your salaries, into a common checking account. There should be a little overage to be used as a savings towards the proverbial rainy day. Whatever is left over from your respective salaries should go into a personal savings account, with yours controlled by you, and hers controlled by her. Let her go to hell with her savings if she wants to. There is but one exception to this approach – and that is the cell phone bill. The both of you need to have separate billing for your respective cell phone bills, paid out of your respective savings accounts. This way, she cannot wreck the household budget by running her mouth on the phone. Mister, you must put your foot down on this.

Chances are, that you could have avoided a lot, of even all of this, if you had done a better job of selecting a wife – seriously. If you were either careful or lucky, you could have found a woman that you have to compete with, or a woman that you do not have to treat like a child. If you are not married, you might want to look at some of the earlier essays on the kind of woman that you do not want to meet.

Look at the Divorce Laws!

And let me add to that title. Mister, you should not just look at the divorce laws, bit all of the family and domestic laws as well. Now, we can try this again. Mister, you should look at the domestic, family, and divorce laws. Got that? Now, let's try this for a third time, with just a little more added in. Mister, you should look at the domestic, family, and divorce laws <u>before you get into any committed relationship</u>. At a minimum, you should have a casual knowledge, at least, of what can possibly happen if things go wrong. After all, you had better believe that she knows what to do, or know somebody who knows what to do, if things go wrong.

Now, what would I call a committed relationship? Well, for me personally, this is a relationship where the man and woman stay together more than 48 hours at a time, and when it is mutually agreed that other potential lovers are out of the picture. Of course, you will have your own idea of what a committed relationship is. You owe it to yourself to research – and then understand – exactly what you are legally getting into once you desire to take your relationship up to another level. If you are already married, you need to get a better idea – as opposed to having no idea at all – of what you may be exposed to, and liable for.

Take a couple hours and do your "due diligence" and research the alimony and child supports laws within the state that you live in. Have a lawyer or a paralegal (preferably a paralegal –they are less expensive) explain to you what the practical applications of these laws are. The goal of this book is to get you men off of the starting line, where you have been standing all of these years. Most of you have been watching women run legal laps around you, and you have had no idea why. The current body of law is huge, and much too much for this book, even if I had concentrated only upon New York state. In addition to that, no two cases are exactly the same. However, there are still some generalities that I can tell you about here.

One of the first things that you need to know is that the entire body of divorce and domestic law is not static. Some states, such as New York and California are seen as "progressive", because they are at the forefront when it comes to passing pro-female legislation. A few states, like New Jersey and Texas, have actually relaxed some of the more punitive statues in their jurisdictions. But the overwhelming content of most domestic law is pro-female, no matter how carefully and gender neutral those laws are written. And these laws can get absolutely draconian at times. For example, in five states, New Hampshire, Virginia, Michigan, Oregon, and Washington State, offer lifetime alimony for women. That's right, I said <u>lifetime</u>. On top of that, your ex-wife is usually able to take something from your pension or estate. Until earlier this year (2014), New Jersey was also one of those "lifetime alimony" states, but they changed the law in May of that year. The state of California is kind of "on the fence" with its' Family Code Section 4336. In this code, any marriage of over ten years is considered a "long term" marriage. Therefore, the divorce court there will retain "jurisdiction indefinitely" over such a divorce. Here also lies the possibility of paying lifetime alimony. Most other states index the length of your marriage to the amount of time that you must pay alimony. As far as the amount of alimony, most states arrive at that amount according to a series of complex questions about your income and her income. New York State uses two calculations. They have a "Calculation A" which uses 30 percent of the payers' (the mans') income, minus 20 percent of the payees' income. Then there is a "Calculation B" which is 40 percent of the combined income minus the payees' income. I do not know who gets which one. If your wife is a stay at home wife, believe me, this is taken into account, and this will increase the amount of alimony that you will have to pay. And this is one thing that will probably never change. After all, there are more women voters than men; and the stereotype of the long suffering, hapless housewife left in poverty will probably never disappear.

However, a closer look at reality reveals something different. With today's millennial generation, more women than men are entering and finishing college. This results in higher overall incomes for women. Today's women have a wider selection of career possibilities as well as help in overcoming any obstacles in obtaining that career diploma. Don't think, for a minute, that today's men will be able to benefit, as a group, from the body of law that the woman has benefitted from all of these years. There are a lucky few men that did benefit; but remember, that's the reason why they are called the lucky few. See the New York State divorce law section 50, below, for why I wrote that.

It makes me wonder then, where in the hell were the state legislators and lawmakers when all of these family and divorce laws were proposed and put up for a vote? Unfortunately, it turns out that that there are certain sections of domestic and divorce law that never would have passed muster if they had been proposed on a stand-alone basis. Many such laws are submitted as part of a larger, more popular bill that is often unrelated to domestic or divorce law, or even to answer a need for such a law. This is what has happened recently in New York State, with the passage of the Woman's Equality Act. This Act is, first of all, an "omnibus" bill, as it carries other legislation behind it. This bill provides for a number of things that range from laudable (more protection for women against sexual harassment in small business) to ridiculous (the right to abort a baby up to a perceived point of viability or six months; and that alcohol and drug use by the victim does not matter when she declares that she has been raped).

All of this really means, mister, is that I must implore you once again that you do at least some research on the laws within your state. You can start out by visiting your state's laws on an official website online. But, be warned, that some of what you see online may be a contraction or an abridged edition of what the law might actually be. Part of the reason for doing this may be space, and part of the reason for doing this just might be to keep men stupid and uninformed. The solution to this is to go down and visit your state's law library, which is usually open to the public. These law libraries are often located within the larger courthouses at the state capital or county seat. You will have to go there and ask the clerk about where your states' domestic and divorce laws are located. And yes, it might seem extreme, and even paranoid to do this, especially when all is well with your relationship. But this is still better than finding out about these laws in the middle of a divorce or child support crisis. Keep in mind that these laws are usually written in a dense legalese, and it takes some understanding of the legal jargon to decipher what these statues mean.

With all of the above in mind, let us move forward and examine just one of the divorce laws of New York State. This particular statue, which is online in its entirety, is from the New York State Domestic Relations law, statue 50, Property of a Married Woman:

> "Property, real or personal, now owned by a married woman, or hereafter owned by a woman at the time of her marriage, or acquired by her as prescribed in this chapter, and the rents, issues, proceeds and profits thereof, shall continue to be her sole and separate property as if she were unmarried, and shall not be subject to her husband's control, nor liable for his debt"

What this all boils down to is that famous phrase, usually uttered by a woman. That phrase is "What's mine is mine, and what's yours is mine". And there it is above, legally in the books. I have heard that phrase as a teenager, from teenage girls, up until the present day, and I've dismissed those words, up until I read that phrase in the law. What that law does for women is that it removes almost all risk of loss of personal property and possessions for a woman who is married or who is contemplating marriage.

Looking at this from another angle, this statue also protects women by shielding the assets earned by them during a marriage, as well as any money that she may have concealed from you.

Finally, keep two more things in mind about this law. One, please take note of just how gender specific this law actually is. This law stands out from almost any other New York law about divorce on the books. This law is for women only. Men cannot benefit from this law.

Second, as a man, your vulnerability as to your own money and possessions remains unchanged.

Look at the divorce laws, mister!

SO, DO YOU WANT TO BE THE FATHER?

So, do you want to be the father?

So, do you want to be the father? Do you envision yourself one day as the dad, raising a family? Do you like the idea of having one or two little ones at your side? Would you like a little toddler, a mini-me, whom you can pick up, cuddle, hold, and eventually show life to? (Don't forget the changing of the diapers). Would you like to be at the head of a warm and happy household, with maybe even dinner on the table? Did I leave out any superlatives?

Well, that world that I have described above actually belongs not so much to you, today's man. More likely, this world would belong to your grandfather. If you, mister, are to achieve any part of that idyllic world above, then you absolutely have to do your homework, as far as selecting a spouse is concerned. That nineteen – seventies dad's paradise is possible to have today, but in the 21st century, it takes far more work than it did "back then". The good news is that most of this work is mental. Let me try and update your thought processes on fatherhood here.

Presently, it seems to me, that both men and women put more thought, and effort into buying a house or a car, than having a child. People need to understand that having a child is a permanent, life-long and life changing decision. If you are a responsible adult, you must accept the responsibility of bringing up this child in a responsible manner. You must continue to do so until, at the very least, the child is able to feed and clothe him or herself. You must do your best, and make your best effort, in raising your child, and in making that child a responsible member of society.

Please take in what I am writing here. I am not talking about money. Too many idiotic people, both men and women, equate fatherhood with an ATM. "Is he paying for the child?" is the first question that they ask when they hear of a couple breaking up. What I am talking about is raising and nurturing the child, especially the male child. Mister, you need to give him someone that he can look up to, both figuratively and literally.

As a man, you need to have all of the above things in mind before you even think of having a child. As a man, you also need to know that any woman that you are having unprotected sex with (not just your "chosen" baby's mother) is actually fit for motherhood. If you feel that she is not, then bag it up! Alternatively, if you are irresponsible, you can take a chance on paying child support (about a 30% chance) for the next 18 to 21 years. Or you can have a child that may have less than a stellar opinion of you. You can find out if she is ready for this new reality by talking to her. However, you, the male, must be aware that many women will lie and claim that they are ready to have a child, when, in reality, they are not. For many of today's women, a child is not just a child. For them, a child is a social-economic football for her to carry, with society and the courts as the potential linebackers. Needless to say, if things go wrong between you and the child's mother, those linebackers will line themselves up against you, the man. Now, you might say to yourself, well, I know that. And perhaps on some level, every American man knows this. But, how many of you American men actually <u>apply this knowledge to your lives?</u> How many of you actually have a condom handy (and not in your wallet) and that you intend to use it if you get lucky? Do you think about this when you are bringing that girl that you met at the bar home tonight?

If you already have children, did you discuss, or were you willing to discuss, with your child's mother, or wife or girlfriend, the prospect of having a child? Was it even a conversation, or did the woman just come in and simply announced "I'm pregnant"? Or, did you just give in to her demands? Even if it was a conversation, how long did that take? A month? A week? Fifteen minutes?

Listen, guys, read this carefully. Among women, what usually happens is this. Your girlfriend, or significant other, when she feels comfortable enough with you or comfortable enough within the relationship, will simply decide to get pregnant. Often, she has had a big discussion about it, but generally, not with you, the prospective father. This discussion took place with her friends, and they all decided together on what course your woman will take. Sometimes, this discussion will include her mother, or even your own mother. Your own mother just might keep that all important discussion hidden from you. American women often don't care about the man's opinion on having children. They reason that it's their bodies and that you, the male, should have thought about that before you slept with her. I am repeating this again because you guys need to hear this again. Returning to that important discussion now, the only hint that anything has taken place might have been when your woman asked you a couple of questions about having children. If you are a busy or an insensitive man, you might have forgotten about that conversation.

Sometimes, a woman might feel differently in her body, and realize that she is pregnant. In this case, that conversation with her friends will happen, but they will focus more upon when they collectively think whenever is the right time to tell you. I can almost guarantee it, mister, that you will not be the second person to find out that she's pregnant. You might be the sixth or seventh person.

In some relationships, your woman might not discuss the pregnancy with you at all. If you and her are close to breaking up, she might simply let you walk out. She might see if there's another guy out there who is willing to help raise the child. If not, don't worry, she will reappear, with the baby, especially if she finds out that you are with someone new. Right after that, the child support authorities may be let loose to catch up with you and wreck your life. But, the larger point that I'm trying to make here is that, again, today's women really do not care about what you, the man thinks when it comes down to having children. Some women don't even want to be bothered with a relationship; they want only to have a baby. Think about that when you come across that hot, older woman. Today's women know that once you pass the sperm, you, the man, really does not have a choice in the matter. In fact, you, the man, may not really have a choice when it comes to fatherhood (as far as visiting and raising the child is concerned. Your only "choice", if you want to call it that, might be to pay for the child, once it is proven that you sired the child (or that you simply said "yes" to a certain question within the courtroom). Listen, I'm serious about this, guys. A man who is not married to the baby's mother has few, if any, legal rights. And going to court in order to exercise those few rights will almost always lead up to paying child support. And, I know that some of you guys will doubt me and think that this is not true, or that you will shake your heads and cluck your tongues, thinking that I am being too shrill or overwrought. Well, mister, it is <u>you</u> who had better wake up and read – and understand this book, cover to cover. Again, I am not being shrill, I am exposing to you the very real possibilities of what can happen to you if you don't manage your sperm or your girlfriend.

Now, let's take a walk on the other side – on the female's side of this baby's equation. It is a reflection of the women's influence on American society that any female has a number of choices as to what she wants to do with a baby. The baby, whether born or unborn, has no rights. There is no "best interests of the child" when we are dealing with females and infants. A woman can freely make choices which are in the worst interests of the baby, without sanction. You can compare this to the male's "next to no choice" when it comes to a baby.

A woman's choices, when she discovers that she is pregnant, starts with whether or not to tell you. She can be honest, and tell you. Again, she can (and most likely will) discuss the pregnancy with her friends. She can discuss with those friends when to tell you so that she can get the best possible reaction. If you are not around, she can have the baby and file for child support later, or from another state. She can forget to tell you, and let the grown child find you, years later. She can refuse to tell you at all, and get an abortion. She can hide the pregnancy from you, and get a partial birth abortion. Let's talk about that partial birth abortion, for a minute. What happens here is that the doctor induces the birth process to the point where only the baby's head is exposed. The doctor then takes a large syringe, and pierces the baby's skull with it. With the syringe, he or she then draws out the baby's brain matter, killing the baby before he or she even has a chance to cry. Then, the doctor withdraws the baby's lifeless body and dumps it in a medical waste bag or sets it aside for medical harvesting at a later date. Think about that for a minute.

We're not done yet. If the mother allows for the child to be born (remember, mister, this is entirely her choice, and not yours) and you are not around, she can simply set the infant into a garbage can, and walk away. Yes, your woman can do this (I'm sorry to have burst your little Ms. Sweet Thing bubble). And, it is not just poor or ghetto women who do this either. Although a woman will generally go to jail for this, most of the time, they get away with it. Indeed, middle class or well–off women are even more likely to get away with this.

Some states, including New York, kind of make infant abandonment "legal" by passing laws that allow pregnant women to give away their newborns to a police station, fire department, or a hospital. While the goal may be laudable in that it may save the life of a baby, it also lets the mother off of the hook; she walks away scot-free, having created a life without having to take care of the baby. Even if the authorities know who she is, that woman will not be charged with child support. That burden is left to society and the taxpayers. But, if the authorities find out if you, the male, are the father of this child, then you will be charged with as much child support as they can legally get.

Finally, she can have the baby with you present, or at least knowing about the birth, or she can have some other man present. Then again, that does not mean you are the father.

Now that the baby is here – whether it was rescued from a trash can or born under a bevy of flowers and fawning mother in laws – a whole raft of laws come into effect. Again, if you are not married, you, the male, have very little in the way of parental rights. Legally, in most states, the custody of the child is presumed to be with the mother. In summary, the goal of all of these laws is to help the baby's mother at the possible expense of the baby, you, the male, and society as well. Believe me, everything that I have mentioned above, is reality. If you, the male, are not careful, it could be your reality. Listen, you can read it here, believe it, and understand, or you can have it told to you at the height of stress and crisis by a lawyer. Yes, it's just that simple.

But, if you, the male, have learned to control your sperm and select your women, this should not be a problem to you at all. And, one other thing. If a woman tells you that she can't get pregnant, she's a liar. She wants to have a baby by you. Don't ever believe her. This is a huge red flag; indeed, you should leave her.

Now, one more time, let's look at this baby thing again, again from her perspective. Having a child, from the woman's point of view, brings to her a series of mostly positive changes, in her eyes. She feels that a baby will always love her, unconditionally. She is wrong; a baby will need to <u>depend</u> upon her, unconditionally. Most women always seems to confuse the two. After she has had the child, her position in society rises up a notch or two. She can count on lots of attention, and she can enjoy this attention because, now she has rights. She can position you to be the horse that will pull her cart all throughout life now, because you, the male, were told to do this. To most people, you are not a man if you don't do this. And if you don't, all of those domestic and family courts laws come down squarely behind her and against you. Imagine having to make this commitment to a woman that you thought would be just a hookup. In any case, the baby's mother is often content to let you think that you wear the pants in the relationship, but the hidden power of the state is behind her and at her beck and call.

So, let me ask you again, do you want to be the father?

What if you are an Unmarried Dad?

Earlier within this book, I wrote about why you should be wearing a condom. I wrote about how you might avoid a number of problems because you wore a condom. But, you guys are hard headed. Your hard headedness might have gotten you into the position that you are in today. How do I know? Because I'm a guy, and, yes, I was hard headed. At least I am writing from a position of knowledge.

Okay. There you are, with your baby and your baby's mother. While the relationship might be OK today, you need to know that whatever happens as far as you and the child is legally concerned depends almost totally upon the mother. She has a number of choices to choose from, and some of those choices will put you at a disadvantage. If you have enjoyed a steadfast relationship with the mother, and the child was expected, well so much the better. If you have had a one night stand, and she has dropped this news of a child on you ten minutes ago at the bar, well, now you have a problem.

Before I get into the legal aspects of all of this, I need to tell you that if you are not or were not serious with the child's mother when it comes to making a place in the world for this child, then the both of you have set the child back behind his peers almost from the start. I've seen hundreds of online studies about children of single parent households. According to just one of these studies, from Wisconsin, stated that of all the delinquent children that they looked at, 44% of these children came from homes where the parents were single parents, or never married parents. An additional 33% of the children came from the homes of divorced parents. This is just part of the effects that divorce has on children. Only 13% came from the homes of two married parents. Now, there is an additional 10% of children but the study claims to not have gotten information on those kids. But, that really doesn't matter. The point that I am getting at here is that you, the male, knowing the potential problems of having an unplanned child is far more important that anything legal. I want you, the male, to understand that you either need to redouble your efforts in trying to properly raise the child, or redouble your efforts in using the condom. There is not much use in talking to the female about this because it seems to me that most females don't really care when or how that they have a baby. They don't seem to mind leaving things up to chance in this area of life.

If you are at odds with the child's mother, legally, you are pretty much out of luck when it comes to having any rights to the child. This does not mean that you are off the hook when it comes to paying for the child. What it does mean is that the mother has the legal right to make any and all decisions about your child whether you like it or not. She can relocate to another state or country. She can go back to an ex-boyfriend (or girlfriend) with your child and have that person act as the father while you pay for that.

In most states, the mother is presumed, from the birth of the child, to have sole legal and physical custody. In these states the unmarried father (even a long time, live-in boyfriend) has no enforceable parental rights.

If you do nothing about this, or if you presently have a good relationship with the mother, you may not have anything to worry about. But, if the relationship goes sour, please know that this is where you stand. If you are on the outs with your child's mother, and you have never "made it legal", then perhaps your only recourse to secure any rights at all is to go to Family court within your jurisdiction and petition for – and prove – paternity. As simple as this looks, in reality, this could be a life altering decision. Before going to court, you should first speak with a lawyer. If you can't find or afford a lawyer then you should consult an objective friend. If you are heartbroken or upset that your child is gone, do not rush into the court without some kind of consultation. Justice for the male from the court is slow in coming and you might not see it at all. Only if you can prove (not just feel) that your child is in danger will you get any quick help from the court.

Do not go to court if you are not the father of the child.

Do not go to court if you are not sure that you are the father of the child.

Why? Any self-declared declaration of paternity by the father for any child in court is generally irreversible, <u>even if it is later proven that you are not the father of the child.</u>

You may become liable for child support for this child until he or she turns 18 years old in, in 45 states, or 21 years old, in five states. Of course, if the child is yours, you are liable for paying child support anyway. But if the child is not yours, do not ever go in front of a judge and pledge paternity if you are not absolutely sure that you are the father of the child. Listen, a woman will lie to you. Even your woman. This happens more often than you think. If you have any doubts at all, then take a paternity test. I do not care what the mother says. After all, about 33% of men find out, through these paternity tests, that they are not the father. Please remember that this is potentially a 21 year decision that you are testing for.

Even if you are not the father, this does not mean that you are out of the woods just yet. In many states, if your child's mother can prove to the court that you, the "father figure", has developed a bond (whether real to the child or imagined by the mother) to the child of over three years, you may still be on the hook for child support.

Now, I can understand, if you are trying to save the child from its' mother, well, by all means you should endeavor to get legal custody for the child. But, if you are simply on the outs or are breaking up with the mother, you should carefully consider the option of going to court. Whatever rights that you might gain as being the legal father can be knocked down by an allegation from the child's mother of domestic violence, or domestic abuse. The issuance of an order of protection can pretty much knock out all of your rights to visit the child.

It would probably be best to try and maintain at least a cordial relationship to the child's mother. Support the child, using checks and money orders made out to the mother. You, the father, would be wise to keep track, and store those money orders or checks in a safe place, for future reference.

PATERNITY FRAUD

Paternity fraud occurs when a mother has a child from one man, and then accuses another man of being the father. She may not be sure of who the actual father is, but she often makes a choice on which prospective father is more attractive (has more money) to her. That man might not be the baby's father. Or it could be that the mother simply has had too many sexual partners, and she really does not know who the father really is. So, she just selects someone, and hopes that he goes along with it. This often works, and a lot of you guys, yes, you, the male, can end up becoming legally liable and end up paying for a child that is not his. This can happen when the mother goes to Family Court and, as they often put it "preys for relief" as in a decision on paternity and child support.

Generally speaking, any woman can accuse you of being the father of the child even when you both know that you are not the father. If you do not want to pay child support for the next 18 to 21 years, you, the male must know, first off, that you should not ever adopt her child. Doing so locks you in and gives you the same obligations as the father. You may not have the same rights as the father, especially if the child has any resentment towards you. In any other case, you will still have to prove that you are not the father. If you have not booked some time on Maury's famous TV show, you will have to pay anywhere from $300 to $500 for a professional DNA test. A home DNA test may not be admissible in court. The financial onus is on you, the male, no matter how ridiculous the accusation may be. If the test proves that you are not the father, you are still out of that money for the DNA test. In most states, you cannot force the mother to reimburse you. As for the mother, there are no costs or expenses that she is liable for. She can even accuse ten men of fathering her child, and be wrong all ten times (again, see Maury's show) and still, there is no cost to her. And the morality of it all? Morality left, on the 5:24 to Oyster Bay......in 1999.

If you are living with a mother and her small child, or children, and you, the man, has helped to raise that child as if it were yours, you can also be liable for child support. Again, the mother can go to the court, "prey for relief", and tell the judge that you and her child has formed a bond. Generally speaking, if you have lived with the mother and child over three years, it can be legally said that you have formed a bond – no matter how that child actually feels about you. This legal "bond", can all of a sudden, become quite real. You can be forced to pay for the child as if it were yours. Listen, guy, I am not kidding, or overstating this. In this way the family courts of all 50 states will uphold, embrace, and enforce paternity fraud. Only the standards or threshold will differ from state to state. Men who have had bad relationships with women who have small children have a significant chance of being forced to pay for these children as if they were the father. And, mister, no matter how much you love the child, do not admit paternity for a child that is not yours. The family court will often try and trick you into admitting paternity so that you can be put on the payment hook.

There was one particularly telling story which appeared in the Sunday New York Times Magazine on November 7, 2009, of a man who did live with a woman and her young child, for several years. Later, that couple broke up, and the mother went back to the biological father of the child and resumed their previous relationship. The man who was not the father of the child felt frozen out of the new relationship, and so he went to the family court in Eastern Pennsylvania to secure visitation rights. This man, while in the court filing papers, made a false admission of paternity, thinking that such an admission would bring him closer to that child. What happened was that the man who was not the father ended up paying child support…..to an intact family!! Now, that couple enjoys the child support paid to them by the one-time boyfriend, who is now, in more ways than one, the odd man out. He got his visitation rights, although, really, a better description would be "pay per view" of a live human being (the daughter). Subsequent trips to the same court to try and reverse their rulings have not been successful. It seems that only men get caught up in things like this.

Yet, recent rulings on gay parents and those families in same sex relationships reveal quite a different set of rules, especially when it comes to women. A New York family court decision rejected the wishes of a Manhattan woman who helped raise a young boy along with his mother. The two had a lesbian relationship and had gotten married in Vermont, then settled in New York as domestic partners (this was in 2009, before legal same sex marriage in New York). The child was conceived by artificial insemination. At the close of the hearing, it was noted that the prospective parent never adopted the child. A lawyer for this child's mother posed this question. "Does someone morph into a parent just because they're living with someone who has a child?" To me, well, the answer is yes – but only if you are male. The hypocrisy is staggering to me. That same lawyer continued with "The law is clear. You're the biological parent or the adoptive parent, or you don't have standing". The woman who wanted to be a parent to this child was denied. This was from a short article in the New York Daily News, of April 11, 2009.

Now, one can say that these are two different cases, in two different states, and at two different times, from several years ago. But this particular facet of family law has not changed much since then. Still, the one thing in common is that there were two persons who fell in love with, and wanted to raise a child with the biological mother, and lost out, because the relationship was no longer needed by the biological mother. Neither person adopted the child in question, although the man was, quite frankly, a fool for signing those paternity forms. The law, in both of these cases, is actually quite clear here. The child's mother always wins. The child does not; he or she is losing out on a parent on whose love might be beneficial. In the case of that man paying to see a child that is not his, imagine him having to swallow his pride, and whatever else, every time he comes to see that kid. So much for the "best interests of the child".

My point here is that men, especially well intentioned men, and usually only men, face many legal pitfalls and liabilities just for settling down with a woman. If you are living with someone, and you break up, you may possibly face almost as many legal pitfalls as you would if you are married. Please take the time to do a little legal research of your state's domestic laws, and find out exactly where you stand in regards to your situation. There are domestic and family laws out there which lie just underneath the "surface", hidden, that apply to nearly every facet of your interaction with women.

For example, in New York, do you realize that if a woman lives with you, after thirty days, you cannot force her out, even if it is your own house and you caught her cheating? You will have to go to Housing Court, stand in line and pay the fees, and wait for a scheduled hearing on the matter.

And, yes, American men, as a group, are fairly ignorant of this. And because they are, I am hollering all throughout this book all of the things that men should know about American, and not just New York's, domestic and family law.

In conclusion, please understand where you stand, mister, in a legal sense, even with something so simple as a live in relationship.

The Duties of the Father Towards the Child

In this essay, I would like to discuss an expanded view of the effects of the father – or the absence of the father – upon the children. This is not about telling you exactly what to do with your child. This is more about what the child should expect from you. I would like to divide this essay into two parts. One is, if you as the father lives with the child as part of the family, and two, if you, as the father does not live with the child. Let's start with the live in father.

As a brand new dad, you must know that the infant, at first, knows no one except its' mother. If you have any doubts about the paternity of the child, now is the time to settle this. Otherwise you should prepare, or better yet, be prepared, to participate fully in the child's life. As time goes by, the infant will grow and learn to recognize other voices that are as familiar and comforting as the mothers'. One of those voices should be yours. As more time passes, your influence will expand, but it will probably not surpass the influence of the mother. That does not mean that your influence is not important. In the coming years your child will watch, and try to emulate, your actions whenever he or she thinks it is applicable. What you say to the child will ultimately mean less than what you do in front of your child. So, you must govern your actions accordingly. Understand that you and the child's mother make up the child's entire world. Most of the child's values and judgments will be set early in life. Over time, others will enter, and then have more limited influence over the child's life. How the child reacts to these people, such as other children or the school teacher, depends on how the child applies the lessons given by you. Therefore it is most important that you be there for your child during the early years. If you are having problems with your wife or girlfriend, please, for the sake of the child, try to hang in there as long as possible, until the child is about ten years old, at least. (If you live in California, better make that nine years). If you break up and leave the household any earlier, the effects upon the child may be life changing and overwhelming. That's not to say that a breakup would not affect a child that's older than ten. Try and look at a breakup from the child's point of view – his or her entire world is breaking up, and he or she will privately wonder whether they had anything to do with it. The child might be afraid to, or choose not to, verbalize their feelings. Then, years later, you will wonder where did they get "that" from when they are teenagers. The more stable your child's world is (world = two parents) the more stable your child will be. It may be exceedingly hard, or even painful, to deal with a non- cooperating spouse, but a separation that is too soon for the child to take will be even worse for that child. And, yes, the child may see you angry, or having an argument, but how you handle that upset will also leave an impression upon the child.

Others have counseled that the parent (usually the female) should breakup as soon as she becomes unhappy, and never mind how the child feels. Those others say those things in order to make the female feel less guilty about initiating a breakup. And, guys, keep in mind that it is the female who most often begins the breakup. I am counseling the opposite, because it makes sense in the long run. I am counseling you, the male, to try to hang in there as long as you can, because the child's well-being, at least in those formative years, is more important than the both you and the mother's happiness.

If you are the father of a small child and you do not live with the child, your job as the father is far harder than the live-in father. First, you need to understand where you "rank" in your child's life. Believe me, it isn't first or second, like you might think it is. It is far more likely that you will actually end up ranking fourth or fifth in your child's life, behind the babysitter, the school teacher, and your baby mother's new man. All of these people will spend more time with your child than you will. Not only that, but your baby's mother may be actively trying to replace your spot as the father with the new man. With all this as a distinct possibility, you, as the natural father will have to redouble your efforts to bond with your child. On visitation day, clear everything else off of your calendar.

During the visitation (some states call it parenting time, but, let's face it, this is visitation) try to make the day all about your young child. Make no reference whatsoever as to what the mother may or may not be doing. The young child will not understand this; the child can only understand that the mother is there for him or her. During the handover, do not respond to any provocation by the mother or her new boyfriend. Often, the mother will use this time to showcase the new man that she is with, in order to make you jealous or angry. If you do feel this way, swallow it. This is not about confrontation; remember that this time is all about your child. Ironically, most women don't even see their hypocrisy when they shout that they don't want another woman around your child. In the interests of keeping the peace, it's better to show up for your visitation alone. At another time, when the child is not present, you can inform your ex that she should not be so fucking insecure and how she feels is really not your problem. You should say this in a sweet, conversational voice, of course.

Sometimes, relations between you and the child's mother may deteriorate to the point where she does not allow you to see the child at all. This is basically "theft of visitation", and the courts, generally speaking, will take a lukewarm attitude towards her actions. The real problem behind this is, you will never get those precious days back. Technically, you are entitled to go to the police station or precinct with your court papers with you, and the police are supposed to enforce the visit. I tried that once, in Brooklyn, with the vaunted NYPD. I went to the police station, where a somewhat sympathetic cop told me that nothing was going to happen there. He told me to go to the mother's address and call 911 from there. I did that, and a woman answered the 911 line. She seemed put out and a little angry that the call was not for an emergency. I told her that a cop advised me to do this. She ended the call by lying and saying "they'll be there right away". Forty-five minutes later I called 911 again, and repeated my problem, this time to a young man. I was able to tell this guy where I was and the color of my car. About twenty five minutes after that, a cop car drove up, and the policeman growled, "you called us?" I explained the situation once again, and handed the cop my visitation papers. A further fifteen minutes passed while the cop examined the papers with his partner. Then, finally, we walked over to the place where my son's mother lived. My son's mother was surprised to see the policeman and lied with the next breath, that, of course I could see my son. The cop walked in to her apartment, and came out a moment later. "Tell him he (my son) doesn't want to see him". I still don't know whether that was true or not. The cop handed me the visitation papers and said, "Well, you lost that one". And he was right. I spent roughly three hours for nothing.

I am not saying that this will be your experience. I really hope that it will not be. But for me, that experience moved me even further away from believing in the system, that's for sure.

Yet, there are a couple moves that are left to someone in a situation like I described about myself above. Indeed, there is always something that a man can do. But now, we are getting into the subject of parental alienation, which is the next essay.

Parental Alienation

At this point, and several other points within this book, you might ask, does this guy (I'm referring to myself, of course) think that there is anything good about being with a female or being a dad? Well, my answer is of course there are good, even great things about being with a good woman and being a dad. The thing is, you do not need me to tell you about those good things. It's my job, within this book, to tell you about those things that can go wrong. And there is plenty that can go wrong. Check this one out.

Parental Alienation is the process whereby one parent, usually the female, tells the child or children that the other parent, usually the father, is bad or unworthy. The question left hanging in the air is, of course, if Dad was so bad, why did Mother decide to have a baby or babies with him? Alas, the children never think to ask that question. Most often, they are too young. Parental alienation is a process that takes place over time, and some mothers start with it as soon as the child is able to communicate. Many mothers believe, correctly, that the earlier they start, the more the child will believe them. After all, would your mother lie to you? There are many forms of parental alienation, and it can occur even if the father is still within the home. The parent that performs the alienation often seeks to have a closer confidence with the kids, even when it is inappropriate to do so. Such a parent, usually the mother, will let the child get away with a small transgression and then say "don't tell your father!" or they will maximize any flaws that the father seems to have. They will often lie outright to the father, even when a lie is not even necessary.

When a parent begins to alienate the other parent through the children, and the father is not or only sometimes present, the children will end up believing without question whatever the alienating parent is saying. These positions will harden over time and may lead to a permanent estrangement of the now young adult from the target parent. I guess you could call this a victory for the mother.

I myself went through this with my own younger son. I caught his mother taking him aside one day and telling him that my older son (from another mother) did not have to be his brother. She also told him that I did not have to be his father. Please note that she failed to tell this revelation to the Family Court. At the time, I thought that what she was saying was ridiculous and that she would be proven wrong through my actions and the actions of my older son (they did get along).

But I was the one who was proven wrong.

Even without any alienation, most mothers blithely assume that the children will be on "her side" and that this will never change. Generally speaking, this is true for pre-teenagers. Older children will develop their own minds. Still, some parents, in their zeal to alienate their children at this age might develop a plot or a plan ("tell the police that he touched you!") in order to secure the children's, and the court's allegiance in the face of an impending divorce.

Again, the results of parental alienation will often vary with the age of the child, and the intensity of the custodial parents' lies, and how often those lies were repeated. A teenager might flat out reject the attempts by one parent to alienate them form the other parent. But if the child was young, he or she may accept the negativity of the alienating parent. It might get to a point that this child may not even be able to look at you without automatically first hearing whatever negativity the mother said about you. If the child grows up this way it will be very, very hard for the alienated parent to form a relationship.

If you are, for example, a father who periodically visits your child or children, and you sense that they are pulling away from you, or that you know outright that their mother is talking bad about you, there is not much that you can do about this. The courts will entertain only the most egregious cases of parental alienation. The best that you can do, for free, is to show your child that you are the better person. You can prove, by your positive actions that the mother is a liar or jealous is the best way to go. Should your child ask you about the subject matter in question, you should try not to overreact. You should explain your views to your child in an age-appropriate manner. You should calmly set out your position, and then ask the child what he or she thinks. Do not use this discussion as an opportunity to attack the mother. The child just might dismiss you as simply the other crazy parent. Try to keep the confidence of the child. After all, the mother usually has far more time to talk to the child about you, than you do about her. Unfortunately, in the end, it is all about what the child ultimately thinks.

But what if you cannot see or visit your child? What if you feel that your child is 100% alienated from you? In this case, you can still do something. You can take a piece of paper – yes, an old fashioned piece of paper – and a pen or pencil, and write down your thoughts about your child or children. After you write down your thoughts, put the date and time on that piece of paper and keep it in a safe place with your personal documents. Don't use a phone for your message to get lost or a computer to let a virus wipe it out. Use your own handwriting. One day, the child may come to see you, if only out of curiosity. When you show your child your thoughts that you wrote down on the now - yellowed paper from years ago, the child will see proof that you at least thought about him or her in the past. He or she may then be forced to at least reconsider their opinions about you.

The Single Father – with an Infant

I am writing this essay for the male who, for whatever reason, finds himself alone with an infant child. Perhaps your child's mother has simply abandoned the child (and you, as well) and, lo and behold, there you are, left on your own with a little baby. Or maybe she is just gone for a while. At this point, there are two things to remember.

The first thing to remember is that you, the male, was probably not raised to deal with the day to day, or even more likely, the hour to hour care of an infant. You might have witnessed your younger siblings as infants, and you might have even stared down, looking at the wriggling baby in the crib. But, it was always your mother or your sisters who pushed you out of the way when the baby needed tending to. Generally speaking, your mother or your sister did not tell what they did nor did they share their knowledge with you.

The second thing to remember, is that you, as the male, and now as a single father, must educate yourself, as fast as possible and as completely as possible, about everything that the baby wants and needs. You have got to turn to, and rely upon, the women in your family to help you out. Usually, the women within your family are only too happy to help you out. This does not mean you can go out and party and leave then holding the baby while you regress to teenage antics. No, sir. Not even if you are a teenager. You are going to stay there and have those women explain to you the how and why of everything that they do, so at some point, you can take over these functions yourself. The only thing that you are <u>not</u> going to do is breast feed the baby (!). If you do not have any family around, find any willing female that will help you. Your girlfriend, if you have (another) one, might feel "put upon" if she is called by you to help you take care of another woman's child. That is how she sees this, unfortunately. If you do not have another girlfriend, this might be just as well. But then, you have to widen your search for help. Ask a female friend, or a co-worker, or your buddy's sister, or even a neighbor if you think that they are cool. Find someone to help you out, at least in the short term, with your baby. Learn from whoever you end up with.

Take the time to get to know your baby. Understand – don't just think – that the baby is helpless. The baby cannot help itself. The baby depends entirely upon you, for survival. For its' life! Therefore, the baby's survival and comfort takes precedence over every other thing in your life, including other relationships and your job, at least in the short term. Indeed, you might have to bring the baby to your job, if it is not a dangerous occupation. Yes, your baby is <u>that </u>important.

Again, take the time to get to know your baby. Your baby's crying is the only way that it knows how to communicate with you. Your baby will crying in a different way, depending on whether it is hungry, or afraid, or soiled, or if it is feeling pain. It is up to you, as a single parent, to learn and find out why and for what reason that your baby is crying. Always hug and comfort your baby. Show the baby love by rubbing its' belly lightly. Keep your baby swaddled in blankets, and kept warm. The baby's first few months of life should resemble how it was in the womb. Get the baby to a doctor to test and see about any allergies that it might have. Let the baby become used to, and comforted by, the sound of your voice. And there is much more to learn after that.

Being left alone to raise an infant is probably the hardest, most nerve wracking thing that you, as a man, will ever do. But, over time, you will adjust. It gets slightly easier, over time. Hang in there.

The Single Father –With a Pre-Teen

This essay is for the man who finds himself in charge of his young child, who might be past the toddler stage, but not quite yet a teenager. If your child's mother has abandoned or left your small child with you, she is doing a grave disservice to the child. I am not saying that leaving the child with you is bad, but depriving the child of her attention and love is bad. Like it or not, the mother is almost always number one within the child's life. It is rough for the child to accept that the mother is gone. And it is traumatizing for the child to realize that the mother has just walked away. Your mission, mister, which you have no choice but to accept, is to take on this new change in your life, and make a whole new life for you and your child, together.

As with a baby, the new and permanent presence of the young child needs to take priority over everything else in your life. You are to ensure that your child enjoys a serene and stable home where he or she can find anchor and continue to grow. Furthermore, you must take some time out and reassure the child that he or she is not responsible for the current situation.

Also as with a baby, you are responsible for the day to day, and the hour to hour needs of the child. You may have to change your lifestyle so that you can develop a routine that your child can depend on and live by. You may have been living a hedonistic lifestyle, waking up at noon, and going to bed at 4 am. Well, with a young child in your life, all that has to go out the window. And the reason why that life has to change is because your child needs to learn the basic routines of life. Your child needs to get up in the morning and have breakfast so that he or she can have a successful day at school. There is also lunch and dinner, of course. But breakfast is most important. A proper routine of rest, a fortified breakfast, a full day at day-care or school, and interaction in the evening followed by an early bedtime is what your child (and you, as well) need to have.

Your goal is to make this happen, every day. Remember, these are the formative years for your child. The habits that the child learns at this stage of life will have a large influence on his or her future life. Remember that this is your child, and that he or she still depends upon you for nearly everything. If you cannot do this, get the child to someone who will, starting with your own parents. Understand that you are placing a burden upon them and they deserve to be compensated. If this is not possible, it is still up to you to find someone who will help you to raise the child properly. Be totally and unsparingly honest with yourself as to whether you can best raise the child or if someone else can do a better job. Again, raising the child properly is your number one mission in life. The child's comfort is to come before your comfort.

You can make this work if you try.

The Single Father – With A Teenager

Generally speaking, this is the scenario that is most likely to happen under which you, the biological father who previously did not live with his child, all of a sudden gets custody of the child. What usually happens is that your child, now a teenager, has caused some kind of trouble or who has begun to resist her authority. Now the mother is no longer willing to put up with this, and she now remembers that the child has a father. She is now ready to remove this child from her life and give him or her over to you. She has probably threatened the child previously with "I will send you to your father!" while they are busy berating the child. And so now it has finally happened, the mother has sent the recalcitrant teenager to you. For her, this child's exile is a relief. It is also a tacit acknowledgement of your role as a disciplinarian.

But, discipline is not really what the newly arrived teenager needs, at least in the beginning. You will have to try and give the teenager a little time and space, to adjust. Take some time to tell the child that you are glad to see them and that you would like to start off with a fresh start together. You might not have any idea of what kind of trouble that it was that got your kid sent to you. When your child – and you – are both comfortable with the new situation, then you can bring up the problem that has brought him or her to you. Don't take any position on that subject for the time being. Try to focus upon the future, and getting your child into a new school, if that is necessary. Then sit down with your child and establish some ground rules, like what time they are supposed to be back at home on a school day or on a weekday. For once, you do not really have to change your lifestyle dramatically for your teenage child – unless he or she can't get out of bed every morning for school.

If you, the father, and your child's mother are not within the court system, try and keep it that way. You should expect the mother to pay for some of the child's expenses, just like she wanted you to do. Don't think that it will happen, though. Few women believe that they should pay for anything. If the mother is still around, you should let her visit. Remember, this is all about the child's well being. But, these visits should only be upon prior notice, and maybe every other weekend, just like they do in court. If the child wants to see the mother more often, let them, so long as it does not interfere with the child's schooling or your own schedule.

If you, the father, and your child's mother are within the court system, you must first be sure – or make sure that the child is going to stay with you permanently. A month long tantrum by the mother is not going to help you. If you are on speaking terms with the child's mother, call her up and discuss with her how the both of you should proceed. If the two of you present a united face at the courthouse, this will get you the fastest possible decision going forward.

If you are not on speaking terms with the mother, then things get a lot harder, even though the child is in your custody. The mother, once in court, can reclaim the child, no matter how the child actually feels about that. If the lies that the mother uses are spectacular or outrageous, she just might get away with using them in court. And, most women are not willing to give up the child support, even when the child is no longer present. To most mothers, child support is money that they "deserve" for the act of even raising a child. There are more than a few women who never really cared about raising a child in the first place.

So, anyway, try to get yourself a lawyer and fight it out, up to and including getting child support from the mother. Do not expect to get a large amount, or sometimes, any amount. A female judge or a male judge who is sympathetic to women will find every excuse to deny you child support from the mother. You, the male, should plan on receiving little to no real help from the mother or the courts, other than getting custody of the child. The courts are often not prepared to help fathers. Yes, I know that the family and domestic laws are written as gender neutral as possible, but my actual court experiences have shown otherwise. When I was receiving child support checks from my son's mother (yes, that happened), I got those checks intermittently, at the mother's leisure. At the New Jersey family court, it took me over a half hour just to convince one clerk that I, the male, was actually receiving child support. No one threatened her driver's license or bank account, ever. Ultimately, you, the father, should take whatever you can get from the courts and the mother, but keep your long term focus upon the child.

SO, DO YOU WANT TO BE THE STEPFATHER?

So, do you want to be the Stepfather?

Alright, so now you are in a relationship with a woman who has young children. The average man, in this position, usually does not give much thought to this situation, beyond the fact that there's another man somewhere who has had children with his woman. The average man might think, well, she is simply a woman with children, a minor complication. Please allow me to give you some thoughts on this subject.

It would be a smart thing for you, the man to do, even before you enter the household of a woman with children on a recurring basis, to find out just how things got that way. This is a question that some men fail to ask. Generally speaking, the mother has anticipated that question a long time ago, and she knows exactly what to say to you – if she has not said it already. She will tell you what she thinks you want to hear. This is not necessarily what you need to know. The truth is, in the beginning of the relationship, you might not have a clue as to how and why the original father left. Well, you can accept what she says, for now. What she says can be accepted as a kind of a "baseline", to be contrasted with what you might hear later.

Even so, you can give some thought about what she might have told you about her previous relationship. Do not question her aggressively on this subject, lest that set off an "alarm" in her head, causing her to lie even more.

You might wonder why you should even bother to do such detective work on your lover. Well, for starters, it makes the difference between you arriving into this new family unit as a true, authentic stepfather rather than someone who is being used as an interloper, or someone who is being used to punish the biological father. Most women who have been recently separated enjoy setting up a revengeful scenario in which the biological father comes to visit the children, only the find another man stretched out on his old sofa and working the remote on his old TV. This new man, relaxing with his big feet on the arm of the sofa where the biological father used to put his head, is now waiting on the dinner that the children's mother never cooked for the biological father. And, that biological father might still be paying for that sofa and that TV, or maybe even the whole house. And while you are chuckling at that, mister, think of the other side of that situation, from the biological dad's point of view. Your sly smile will instantly disappear when you realize, entirely too late, that there are some fathers who won't stand for that, and this father is going to blow your head off with the gun you never thought that he had. Please note that I said he will blow your head off, not the mother's or the children's' heads.

Now, do you understand the need to do at least some research into this new family unit? Did you listen carefully to the mother's explanation of how they broke up? How does she frame the previous relationship? Has she called the man out of his name (That bastard....''), or expressed satisfaction at having called the police to remove him, or involving the courts to sanction him? How do the children feel about their father? Did they even know him? Do they miss him? If some or even one of these answers is not to your liking, then you might want to ask yourself if you are moving in too soon. You might want to ask yourself if the war between the mother and the father (or, even the previous man) is actually over. If that war is not over, do you think that you should be there at all? (hint: no).

Women are very, very good at presenting themselves as the victim, no matter what really happened. They can "gas" you or fill you with anger by portraying themselves as defenseless waifs pitted against a raging oaf or doofus. They don't want you to understand why this man is so angry – but they know why. By the way, women also "gas" the police and the judges the same way. Have you ever heard or seen a woman say what she did before the problem or fight started, even on those talk shows? (He just came in and started hitting me......") For a woman, it is always, always what he did, and never what she did. She might have been caught sleeping with his best friend. The judges, the police, and now you, the "new" man, are all ready to act on that, without knowing exactly why, and without asking why. All you guys know is that the man who hit her must be taken down. And, the more "traditional" or "manly" that you are, the further you'll go on her "gallon" of "gas". Are you one of those guys who feels that you must defend your woman's honor? Are you even defending her honor, or just some whispered accusations? Be warned that if you find yourself in this position of defending her against the previous man or the biological father of the family, the mother will expect for you to be violent; she anticipates that you would fight and defeat this man. And, yes, this is the one time that a American woman would encourage and expect domestic violence. And this is the one time the courts might let you get away with it. But, be warned again. If you lose the fight, or worse, if you refuse to fight, you will no longer be a man in her eyes. She will lose respect for you, and look for another man that will fight.

My advice? Refuse to fight. It does not really matter what she thinks of you anyway. In her mind, she was using you to get back at the biological father anyway. Imagine getting hurt or injured.... or facing that gun...or ending up in jail.....because you volunteered to be her gladiator.

Now, admittedly, the scenes that I have described above are relatively rare, and extreme, but it does happen. And, sometimes, events can get ahead of you. It is much better to read about it here, than having to react to it out in the street.

There are actually a whole range of possible living situations when you enter into a woman's house with her children. And, there are a whole range of possibilities as well. But, in any case, a positive beginning still does not absolve you of your responsibility -- to yourself – of finding out as much as you can before moving into that household. Moreover, a positive living situation with the mother is not enough here. You, as the man, need to assess and understand the true reaction of the child or children to your presence. The children really are more important. After all, your shared goal with the mother, and you as the stepfather, is to provide an improved environment for the children. This is something to keep in mind when you "sign on" to be with a mother with children. So, you should do your own research, and talk to the children. Find out how they feel about your permanent presence in the household. If the children's response differs markedly from what the mother has said, well, that's a big red flag. The mother's lies – or the children's lies -- are a bad sign for the future of this relationship. That someone needed to lie is not good at all. Frankly, this should be considered a deal breaker.

Keep in mind that, as a stepfather, you will not have a lot of influence within this new family, at least at first. You will also not have a lot of rights, as well. As for your obligations, well, that will be determined by the children's mother. Please be aware that, over time, your obligations will increase, on both a human and a legal level. After three years, you might be obligated to pay child support, should you subsequently break up with the mother.

One final thought….when men are so eager to "step up" and become a stepfather to another man's children….doesn't this diminish the importance of the father in the first place? I already know that the American woman thinks that way. She would be aghast if mothers were replaced at the same rate that fathers are. Just something for you, mister, to keep in mind.

What is a Father Figure?

What, really, is a "father figure?" I've heard that term bandied about a lot, mostly by women who recognize that their sons might need a male in his life but don't really want to deal with a man. They have gotten rid of the biological father but they know that, somehow, somebody has to teach their son to "be a man". As far as I can tell, a father figure is someone who approximates, but does not replicate, the role of the father in the lives of the children. In the minds of most American women, the so called father figure can be male or female. The father figure might even be the provider within the household, but this person does so quietly, so as not to upstage the mothers' presumed role as the head of the household. A father figure might even buy little Jane and little Johnny new shoes, but he does not dare to discipline them. A father figure does not really do anything with or for the children that the mother would not approve of, of even think of. For example, the father figure would, of course, take little Jane to the beauty pageant. He (or she) would not even think of taking little Johnny to the construction site to see how the cranes and trucks work.

So, a father figure is someone who might play the role of "dad lite" or "pseudo dad", mainly as a convenience to the mother. These are the people that replace you, mister, after you have been removed or have otherwise left the household.

To be clear, I am talking about the kind of father figure that comes within a boyfriend that stays around for a while, but not long enough for the kids to remember his name, or the limited lessons he might have tried to teach to the children. If there is an uncle or other male family member willing to be there for the children in the long term, then the term "father figure" might have some weight and meaning. More often than not, it doesn't.

From the mothers' point of view, the father figure is a great asset to have. With a father figure, the male child can learn some of the lessons that he needs to learn in on his way to growing up to be a man. However, exactly what lessons, and whether these lessons are good or bad, are left up to chance.

Another plus for the mother is that a father figure can be removed or exchanged at any time, and at her convenience. Should the child become confused, or has become close to the previous father figure, well, this can be remedied with a slap across the child's face, and a stern "Don't you talk about Mr. So-and-so anymore, alright!" The mother says that this relationship is no more, and she said it, and so it is. Right? Yes, she is right. Mister So-and-so better not say another word to that child, lest he be branded as a child molester. Then again, there are those father figures who just might be unforgettable. There are those father figures whose impressions upon the child just might be indelible, for life. Such as, the neighborhood drug dealer. Or the gang leader.

The Stepparents' Effects Upon The Children

A lot of adults, both male and female, tend to forget about or dismiss the effects of their actions upon the children. The parent and stepparent often forget that the child, of either gender, will watch and learn from what the parent and stepparent <u>DOES.</u> What the parent or stepparent tells the child what to do has less of an impact on them. In this essay, I'm going to focus upon mainly upon the male child. It seems to me, that boys are affected more often, and deeper, by the actions of the stepfather, since it is usually the biological father that leaves, or is removed from, the family home.

Assuming that the boy knew his dad before you left, you, the prospective stepfather (and you might be the prospective stepfather whether you are there on a one weekend stay, or forever) is pretty much the last person a boy wants to see with his mother. This is because you, the new male, might be perceived as a sort of "competitor" for the mothers' love and affection. Or, the boy just might not approve of another man being together with his mother. On a certain level, the boy realizes that you can reach his mother in a way that he cannot. Whenever the boy has to confront this reality, he might not even know how to verbalize his feelings and talk with his mother about it. Even if the boy could tell his mother, he might face being shouted at, slapped, or even suffer a beating at the hands of his mother. That boys' anger or resentment at his mother, or you, the new man, or both of you, will not go away. That boys' anger may manifest itself somewhere else, like in his behavior at school, or his schoolwork, or in his interaction with others. I used to bring this subject up with whatever girlfriend I happened to be with at the time. Their retorts were nearly universal. They would say "he'd better get used to it" or "he'd better mind his business". Sometimes, the women would sound off with things that men used to say, such as "I'm the one who is paying the bills here" or even "I don't care what he thinks – he'd better do as I say!" And all the single mothers would say all of those things with raised voices. No, I have not interviewed every single mother in the universe, but I am pretty sure this is how most of them think. The point is that you, the man should know, is that the single mother is mentally hurting her son each time a new man appears in the household. The single mother may not know this, or she may not even care. This is too bad, because the mother will be, for better or worse, the prototype for most of the women that young boy will meet later on in life. Many of his judgments about women will be formed by his experiences watching his mother. It is funny, no, actually tragic, that women can look at every facet of a boy's life and yet <u>ignore</u> their own negative contribution to the young man's upbringing. If the boy's mother is a disappointment, then many of the women to come later on in the boy's life will be a disappointment. If the young boy sees his mother as a whore, then the women who will follow will be perceived as whores. Again, why women, as a group, fail to see or understand this as an important part of motherhood, I, myself cannot understand.

Feminists, of course, are silent on this subject. It is not the fault of the rap or hip-hop music or even the violent video games that makes a lot of today's young men think that way. Those songs and those games are just the symptoms of the malaise. It is the failure of many single mothers to properly raise their sons that is causing a lot of the dysfunction in today's young males. It is not just me saying this; some of the rap songs are saying the same exact thing. Some of Eminen's songs are very clear.

Listen, I am not trying to be old fashioned, although being old fashioned is not necessarily a bad thing. This view about how mothers play an important part, positive or negative, in a child's life is not old fashioned. This is just an honest truth. It's just an observation that has been passed down from family to family over the years. It is an inconvenient truth to those who always have the excuses in their mouths. Finally, it is part of something that used to be called morality. But we all know that morality has departed on the 5:24 train to Oyster Bay, back in 1999. And guess what Dads? The same thing applies to you. Stand up for your daughter. Even if, for many people, that faded, old fashioned word called morality, has disappeared down the tracks and around the curve.

You, the new man, should think about all of these things before you are ready to come into someone's household and put on the stepfather's crown. As you appear on that scene, you don't really know if you are the first new man to come into that household or the tenth. Once you are in that household, you should step lightly. Keep in mind what I said about the young boy and his anger earlier. You should acknowledge the children; especially the male child. Don't force yourself upon the children but hear what they have to say. Let that male child set the distance between you and him.

Once, I was in a relationship where I was dating a woman who had a teenage son and an 8 year old daughter. While I was able to speak often with the 8 year old, the teenage son kept me at arm's length, with barely a nod. Ass the lucky stars would have it, one of that teenager's friends was the son of a friend that I knew. One day, I asked the teenager's friend why was this teen so distant from me. His reply was "It's not just you. He's that way with all of the guys who are seeing his mother". It actually took me a few minutes to realize that "all the guys" were seeing that teenagers' mother at the same time that I was. Previously in this book I wrote about doing some "detective work" when meeting a new woman who has children. This is what I was referring to. It is simply listening to some – just some – of the things that people who are around your new girlfriend say. But you must be certain that there is some fire to match the smoke that some people put out.

I'm going back, now, to communicating in general terms, rather than personal experience. If your relationship with the child's mother moves along in a positive manner, I still believe that you should not try to take the place of the father of the child. The child's mother probably prefers that you do not try and take the place of the father. What she prefers is that you become the father figure, like I had stated earlier. This way, you can be easily switched out for another man, should that become necessary.

I say this, mister, because at this point, you probably still don't know whether the biological father has walked away, or is being kept away. You should never, ever issue a judgment or remark about the children's father in their presence. It is not your place to do that. The children might have fond memories of their biological father. And, one more thing. Do not adopt the child. There are many other options thru which you can prove your love towards the child besides adoption. And why should you not adopt? Because, with an adoption, you become responsible for the child, as if it was yours, biologically. This means that you will potentially be on the hook for child support and medical expenses, if you ever break up with the mother. Indeed, you still could be on the hook, if you have spent more than three years in this family unit. Then, some courts will declare that you and the child have formed a bond, which also leaves you on the hook for child support.

On the other hand, what if you had formed a genuine, bond with the child, and then you break up with the mother, and now the mother wants nothing to do with you, not even for child support? Well, the mother, and society as well, expects you to instantly forget about the child, and all that had transpired between the two of you. The child is expected to forget about you as well. Society also demands that there be no relationship between you, the man, and the child. If you continue to see this child, you might be branded as a pedophile, which is the worst possible label that American society can throw at you. Yes, a pedophile is worse, in most people's eyes, than a murderer. I don't agree with severing a positive relationship with the child, but frankly, I do not know of any alternatives. The effects of breaking a positive bond that the child had with an adult is not considered by the mother or American society.

THE FAMILY COURT –
AND CHILD SUPPORT

About the Family Court

There are many facets of business within the Family Court. And the Family Courts are different in every state. All sorts of problems that center upon the family and children are dealt with within the Family Court. But here, within this book, we will narrow our focus to those parts of the court that are mostly likely to affect men and fathers. It does bear repeating that some of the decisions and changes that are demanded by the court in the areas of child custody and child support are negative and life-altering.

At the beginning of this book, I began to relate to you what it was like to begin to go through the process of paying child support through the courts. In that essay, I had expressed my bewilderment about the fact that I was even summoned to the courthouse. After all, I had thought, I was no wife beater or deadbeat dad. But, by now, if you were reading this book, everyone should know that you don't have to be "that kind" of a person to end up in trouble and court. And since that time, of course, I have learned a whole, whole lot more. So much so, in fact, that I have learned enough to write a book!

Within this essay, I will try to give to you an unconventional, but accurate view as to the purpose an general direction of not only the family court, but the divorce and domestic laws as well.

So, allow me for a minute, to divert away from my continuous warnings and cautions about the Family Court. This is where the unconventional part comes in. This general overview reflects the current state of domestic, divorce and family laws, and the courts that enforce these laws. After that, I will get very specific about what a man can expect from the court.

The unconventional explanation is this. Perhaps the number one thing that the American woman wants is to be loved, unconditionally. This is, on its' face, not so different from what any other woman on the planet wants. However, this American variation of unconditional love must also provide for her security. And this is not just the security of being with someone. After all, most of the other women in this world also want security within their relationships. But now, this American variation wants even more security for the woman. The American feminist- based goal is to <u>insure</u> that security for the American woman at any price, even at the expense of men, children, and society. And in what form is this security? Money, of course. Money is the American's woman's definition of security. And the American woman must not only have money. She must also have the power of victimhood over the man who she feels has done her wrong. She must also satisfy her unquenchable thirst for revenge. She must see that this man who has left her get plowed under. The American woman is satisfied that she has the power to do this at any time within the relationship. Yet, some of them want more.

This is the background, indeed, this is the base upon which the divorce and family courts operates. Feminists (again, not just women) have been able to change the direction of the courts, law by law, practice by practice, to not just achieve equality, but to achieve dominance, over men.

When you decide to take a look at the divorce and family court systems through the prism of what I have described above, then most of what these courts do finally begin to "make sense", so to speak.

The Legend of the Deadbeat Dad

One of the biggest misconceptions out there is that there is this huge legion of deadbeat dads running around and living high off the hog. These guys, according to some, are running around wild and free in their tuner cars, tossing beer cans out of the car windows, and having a good time. Meanwhile, there is a trail of broken hearted women, with their wailing babies who have no choice but to go on the public dole. One can just see those mothers now, in their patched dresses and their forlorn child, just one diaper away from bathroom oblivion. Most American men and women believe all of the above, without qualification. And this is part of the reason why that the American male is positioned where he is.

Let me offer this truism, in rebuttal. Generally speaking, American men, as a group, have not really changed over the years. Like I have said elsewhere in this book, men have never been liberated. The American man has always defined themselves, and are so defined by women and society, on how well they can provide. Rare is the man that does not brag about what he has, or can do, when prompted. Almost as rare is the man who does not redouble his efforts to provide when a mutually planned – I said mutually planned – baby is on its' way.

Are there men who cut and run? Yes, of course there are. And, are there women who decide to have a child unilaterally? Yes, of course there are. This is where the problem lies, although you will never hear this from a woman or the media. Problem with pregnancy of with a child between a man and a woman often happen when the woman has made a unilateral decision to have a baby. This happens most often when the mother has failed to bring about, or just does not care at all, that the father has an emotional connection to the child. Often, the mother has tasked the unborn child to do what she has been unable to do – trap, or rope the man in, and force him to settle down and marry her. Or, the mother may simply have wanted to have a baby, no matter what the circumstances may be. She does not care that she is darkening the future of this child, by her actions.

At the same time, the man is not entirely off the hook either. His fateful combination of exaggerations and lies to get unprotected sex has helped to get himself trapped with a prospective child that he has no emotional connection to.

But the larger problem here is not the deception of either the mother or the father. The larger problem is, really, the effects of this out of the gate dysfunction upon the newborn baby. Yet, this larger problem is roundly ignored by American society because this truth is not useful to American women and

American feminists. It is more useful to American woman to make the American man, as a group, wrong. It is more useful for the American woman to portray herself, yet again, as the victim. And so, this stereotype of the deadbeat dad survives, and so does the state and federal legislation and laws that are tailored to punish men.

But what about the child? One might ask. Well American society simply does not care about the child as much as the woman. Simply put, no one really cares. The American woman, as seen from the state laws, simply holds up the child as a pimping object to get money from the man, pure and simple. In reality, the child is simply left to negotiate that maze of early life with a single parent, and half – or less than half – of the advice or direction that he or she really needs.

And so, we have that stereotype of the deadbeat dad, alive and intact, and which can be applied to any man, even you, mister (please read the essays about child support) because it is actually the state, through its' feminist based laws and statues, that determines who a deadbeat dad is. Truth and circumstance do not matter here because the American woman wants it that way.

What is Child Support, Really?

That is not a stupid question. Seriously, the asking of what child support really is, can be enlightening to those who are able to pull their heads out of the sands. Let us start with the meaning of child support as given by a popular online dictionary. The given meaning was "in family law and public practice, child support is an ongoing, periodic payment made by a parent for the financial benefit of a child following the end of a marriage or other relationship". Well, that is a pretty good, straight line definition of what child support is actually supposed to be. But the reality speaks otherwise. I have already written about what the real purpose of the divorce and family courts are within the previous essay in this chapter.

Mister, please consider this. In all 50 states, all of the child support checks that are sent out from the state to the custodial parent have only the mothers' (and yes, sometimes the fathers') name on it. In all 50 states, the child's name is NOT on the check, even as a reminder as to where that money should go. In all 50 states, there is no provision (or even a request!) to have such a check deposited in an account for the child's benefit. In all 50 states, there isn't even a requirement to spend child support on the child! And so, we are definitely seeing the "spread" between the dry definition, and the reality of child support. Perhaps we can move away from the core meaning of the words "child support". Perhaps we can substitute the words "mothers' pimping money" or "pussy tax" (a woman suggested that last one). Nevertheless, there are plenty of stupid men out there who actually believe that every penny of child support is spent on the child, just because of the words "child support". Those words have been most useful to the American woman, like the words "rape", "victim", and "predator", to name a few.

Getting back to some men now, these guys actually believe that the child's mother will be inherently honest. They also believe that the more child support that you pay, the better off the child will be. If you are one of those people, mister or miss, please, put this book down, go to the nearest wall, and bang your head against that wall, violently, just a few times. Then, come back to this book.

You can consider this next point with a headache, because I had mentioned it earlier. In New York State, and in many other states as well, only the money that the father (or the non-custodial parent) pays directly to the state is considered child support. Any money that the father actually pays to or for the child is considered by the state as a "gift" and it does not count towards the child support so long as the court order exists. And, please understand that 95% of the people in this position are fathers. So, in addition to having to pay that child support bill, plus the arrears, which are almost always there in the first year, and maybe some alimony as well, you, the non-custodial father, will have to somehow and someway have to get up yet more money to try and cover up to 21 years' worth of Christmases, birthdays and other incidental spending, just to keep pace with the relationship with your child.

Now that your headache has cleared, you, mister or miss, needs to understand that the financial overload and destruction of the male is absolutely by design and not by happenstance. A side benefit (or even a full benefit, depending on the woman) is to be able to sit back and have the state destroy your ex husband or boyfriend for you. It is the rare or lucky middle class man who is able to overcome the setbacks dealt by the divorce and family courts.

And, do not expect the mother to do the right thing with that child support money except to profit off of the child. Most American mothers see child support as a salary paid to them for raising the child. You will probably never see the mother who has put money aside for the child or otherwise budgeted the child support money for the child's future. In her mind, that's still your job. What this means, mister, is that you will probably have to pony up for your child's future college education as well.

So mister, you now have more of a reality based definition of child support.

How Child Support is Calculated

Previously, I have given to you the background in which the New York family court operates in. My goal in doing this was to give you an idea about the atmosphere of the place if you have not been there. I also wanted to give you a general background of the legal atmosphere that you might find yourself in.

But let us now get into the heart of it all; let's get into the numbers and amounts of child support, which is Byzantine in its' workings. I will try to clarify, as best as I can, exactly how this works, in New York State anyway. But no two cases are exactly alike. The goal of all this is to just give you a rough idea of what really happens, and what a lot of the people who have been there are bitching about.

This process is backed by the New York State Family Court act of 1989, statues numbers 413, 416, 433, 438-440, 442-447, and article 5-B. Quoting each statue as it applies here would make things unnecessary complicated. There is enough complication to follow, trust me.

To compute this in the easiest way, I will assume that there are no issues with the paternity of the children. I've set aside examples for one, two, and four children here.

Most New Yorkers have heard, and it is true, that the child support percentages begin at 17 percent of your salary for one child. Then, it goes to 25 percent for two children, 29 percent for three children, 31 percent for four children, and "no less" than 35 percent for five or more children. The source for that information is the "Child Support Standards Chart" (of March, 2014), issued each year by the New York State Office of Child Support Enforcement.

But gentlemen, pay attention! That 17 percent does not sound like that much right now. That 17 percent, and all of the other percentages, is figured out of your gross income, before taxes! That 17 percent is calculated ONLY AFTER the two largest taxes, the State and Federal payroll taxes, are added back on top of your net (what you bring home) paycheck. Only the smallest tax, such as the FICA or Fed MED/EE, remains as a deduction that is still figured in to the states' calculation. The actual deduction from your net paycheck of that so-called 17 percent is more like 25 percent. A child support order for two or more children can seriously hurt your finances to the point of bankruptcy, in short order. And, by the way, going bankrupt does not affect your child support amounts or frequency of payments. Take a look at the "What to do" essay later on within this chapter.

Let us now get into the numbers and amounts of child support, which have an (anti-) life all of it's own.

For clarity's sake, I will assume that your salary is $1,000.00 per week ($52,000.00 yearly) straight salary. You live in New York City ($$$ taxes). In other words, the worst case scenario. Also, I threw in a flat deduction of $75.00 that might have been for a 401(K) or a 457(K) retirement plan, or a savings account, or a health benefit deduction or even union dues. Most people have one or more of these deductions in their paychecks. The total amount is $75.00, which in fact is a little light. Most deductions of this kind are actually more, in most cases.

What follows now is a series of examples of what will happen to that $1,000.00 weekly salary. I will use examples with one child (17pct.), two children (25pct.) or four children (31pct).

In the first example, we will look at your salary, as it is now, before going to court:

1. Your weekly salary $1,000.00
   Minus fed, state taxes 25%   250.00
   All other taxes 5% (FICA, SSI, etc)   50.00
   Deductions 7.5%   75.00

   Real life after tax income (net)   625.00

For the purposes of child support, the Federal and State taxes, and the deductions, are added back in. Only the FICA and SSI taxes are deducted here. In this example, your salary for court purposes is $950.00. The child support deductions are based on that amount.

In figure two, we will deduct the child support amounts, by percentage, of that fantasy $950.00 amount.

One child (17pct.)	= 161.50
Two children (25pct)	= 237.50
Four children (31pct)	= 294.50

Now, let's go back to the real world and see what these deductions look like when they are applied to your real world salary. Remember, in this example, your real life after tax salary is $625.00.

Net salary	$625.00		$625.00		$625.00
Ded./1 child	161.50	Ded/2ch	237.50	Ded/4ch	294.50
Leftover	463.50		387.50		330.50
Actual pct.	(24pct)		(38pct)		(47pct)

At first glance, these amounts might be bearable if you only have one child. But any more than that, you are going to have a problem. And look at the actual (roughly calculated) percentages that child support actually costs! The deduction for one child is really 24 percent, not 17 percent. And the cost for four children is a whopping 47 percent, not 31 percent, of your actual after tax salary. Your "Leftovers" are really leftovers! But, we are not finished yet! Because most cases within the family court consist of more than one visit, and because the calculated amount of money will actually start from the day that she walked in the court and filed (started) the case, there will usually be an arrears amount. The calculated goal of having an arrears amount is to create a financial windfall – almost a bounty – for her. It is also calculated to make a financial emergency for you, to satisfy her thirst for your demise. The arrears are usually half again of what the ongoing child support amount is. So, let's go through that exercise.

Net salary	$625.00		$625.00		$625.00
Ded/1 ch.	161.50	Ded/2ch	237.50	Ded/4ch	294.50
Arrears	80.75		118.75		147.25
Leftover	382.75		268.75		183.25
Actual %	(38%)		(57%)		(71%)

Now, mister, are you finally seeing why this man wrote this book? Do you now understand what some other men are bitching about? Do you think that you can live this way, with 38, 57, and even 71 percent of your salary gone? Can you take that hit on your check, from one week to the next? Can you live this way for years at a time? Those earlier percentages of child support that I quoted first, with 17 percent for one child, 25 percent for two children, and 31 percent for four children, now seem a long, long way from the 38, 57, and 71 percent of your money that is now gone, as shown here. You never hear about what really happens because men, as a group, internalize their anger and pain. We don't want to called out as a deadbeat dad, even at the price of our financial lives. And by the way, fellas, these amounts DO NOT include alimony. But, pay attention - we are STILL not finished yet. There actually is a way – sort of – to keep from having all of your money taken away from you. If you have a good lawyer, he might be able to mention it in the courtroom as you are going down in flames. Otherwise, you will have to apply for it, and what the state wants from you then is even more onerous. This thing is called the "Self-support reserve" wherein the man is "granted" some of his own money to live on. The self-support reserve is set at one hundred thirty five percent (135 percent) of the federal poverty level for one person. This is the level at which they expect you to live. For 2014, the self-support reserve was $15,755 for the whole year. This works out to $1,312.91 per month. In New York City this basically works out to a rented room with a bathroom down the hall and cans of tuna fish. This amount works out to $302.98 per week. Remember that some months have five weeks. Again, let us look at the tables to see how you will fare if the self-support reserve applies.

Net salary	$625.00		$625.00		$625.00
Ded/ 1ch		Ded/2 ch.		Ded/4ch	
w/arrears	242.25	w/arrears	356.25	w/arrears	441.75
Leftover	382.75		268.75		183.25
Self-Sup. Res.	302.98		302.98		302.98
Leftover	382.75		302.98		302.98
	(79.77)		(+34.23)		(+119.73)

Let me explain that last table, a little bit. When the self-support reserve is applied, and you have one child, you actually come out ahead. You have still have $382.75 left, which is $79.77 more than the $302.98 floor of the self-support reserve. This move is unnecessary with just one child. But if you have two children, it becomes necessary. Normally, with the arrears, you would have $268.75, which is $34.23 less than the $302.98 floor. With four children, you would normally have $183.25, which is again now $119.73 less than the $302.98 floor of the self-support reserve.

However – and this is a big "however" – the money that you save with the self-support reserve does not just disappear into the thin air. That money still has to be paid; it simply gets added back into your arrears amount. These arrears can be applied on top of your regular child support payments in increments as little as $5.00 per pay period. It might take you from two to five years to pay off an arrears amount this way.

And there are additional measures that the child support agency can take – please see the next essay.

Well then, doesn't this sound like a lot to go through? Yes, it is. I wanted to bring through to you, the entire mechanics of the child support system, as practiced in New York State. You see, it is not just about the money. It is about using money as a legal sledgehammer. It is about a new kind of indentured slavery, actually.

Alternatively, the child support hearing officer or magistrate can simply turn once again to the Child Support Standards chart. Inside, this booklet shows what amounts should be deducted from your salary, in yearly amounts ranging from $0.00 (the deduction is $300.00!) or $5.76 per week up to $199,999 (the deduction is $33,983.00 or $653.51 per week). Above that amount, it is up to the judge. These are the amounts for just one child.

For our sample salary of $52,000 per year, the chart has, as follows; for one child, $8,840 per year ($170.00 weekly), for two children, $15,080 per year ($290.00 weekly), and for four children, $16,120 weekly ($310.00 weekly).

And yes, the amounts are different from those that I have used in my earlier examples. Then, I had calculated by the percentages. Now, I am quoting directly from the Child Support Standards booklet. I guess that you can call this "the spread".

How Child Support is Collected

Let's take a breather for a minute, especially if you have just finished reading the last essay. I know that I am riding hard, but the reality is hard. The reality is that as I write this, I remember all that I had to go through simply to keep from being deemed a criminal. The reality is, is that the present system will aid and abet, by design, the desire of the child's mother to see a man get plowed over. The reality is, is that I look at my children today and realize that they are not living up to their potential, in part because of all the times that I could not be there for them. And I had to spend a lot of time just wondering how I was going to stay afloat.

But people often say, well, you should have used protection. Nobody told you to go out and make a baby! Well, this is true. But, having made the baby, does the father deserve to be punished for years on end? Doesn't the mother also deserve judgment and punishment as well? Even after she has neglected the children? And there are two more realities to consider. As a father, and as a parent, you cannot give your all to the children without saving something for yourself. And what is that something? It is whatever; it is love, time, money, sanity, and discipline. I know that this is at odds with what most men and the rest of society thinks. The other reality is that the court system represents what the American woman wants over nearly everything else: money.

Anyway......after the court is done with you, at least in New York, you will be issued an Order of Support. The Order of support will stipulate how much you must pay, where you must pay it, and at what intervals. Normally, the money you must pay will eventually be deducted from your paycheck.

Your case, and a copy of the Order of Support, now goes to an entity called the Office of Child Support Enforcement. This is a part of the New York City's Human Resources Administration. In other counties within the state, and in other states, such an office remains under the jurisdiction of that state. The singular goal of this entity is to collect money for child support. The Office of Child Support Enforcement has the power to suspend your driver's or professional license, apply a lien to your property if you have any, empty your bank account, and deny or suspend your passport, all with the purpose of getting your money for child support.

The people who work in the Office of Child Support Enforcement are, almost to a woman, a gallery full of man-hating bastards, whose fervent Taliban-like goal is to make sure everyone else is a bastard. These are people who are often drunk with their power to threaten and abuse men who are charged with paying child support. Most of the women there would work the job for free, just so that they could get their thrill of fucking with men. I am completely serious about what I am saying here; my description is apt. Just ask any man who has been there.

In addition, the Office of Child Support Enforcement will often perform false arithmetic when it is calculating child support arrears amounts. The math done by them will always veer towards more money, never less, in order to increase the financial pressure and sense of turmoil upon the father. They will ignore court orders to return overpayments that may be due back to you.

You have the right to check the math and challenge their assertions. You can do this by mail. However, chances are that whatever proofs that you might have sent will be ignored, or turned down flat.

There is also an office in lower Manhattan where you can visit and see someone face to face to try and solve your problems. However, the people who work there, both women and men, are openly in contempt of men and fathers. Again, most of the women who work there would do the job for free, just to enjoy your pain. These women automatically empathize with your unseen child's mother, and they will do little or nothing to help you, just like the woman who once told me that they did not receive any payments from me. She could not know because she didn't even turn the computer screen on. I guess that they reason that because you are disputing your payments, you are also disputing your fatherhood. And because you are disputing your fatherhood, you are disputing your status as a man, and therefore, you deserve no respect. There are men who work there as well. Most of these are carefully chosen men who were born in other countries where the social stereotypes about men are even more entrenched. They, too, will take a perverse enjoyment of your pain. Many of these people believe even more so that fatherhood = money paid, and why would any upstanding man would want to renounce his fatherhood? Some of them literally believe that you, the father, are actively trying to starve your own child by disputing your child support. A father should be ashamed for even having to be there.

The one or two American males who might actually care to help are hard to come by. And this is all by design.

Everything, and I mean everything above, including the characterizations, that I wrote above about the New York City Office of Child Support Enforcement, I have witnessed personally. There is no need for embellishment.

Mister, at this point, you need to understand that you have simply been reduced from what might have been a full fatherhood to simply a wallet. No one from the state will ever ask, or care, about the relationship with your child. Only the child will care. The state, and your child's mother will only see you as a wallet. You are only as good as the money that you produce. Actually, that last sentence brings to mind another, better analogy. You, mister, are now the whore (or ho'), and your child's mother and the state are co-pimps. Again, you are now only as good as the money that you put out. Not only that, but you must put out that money for up to 21 years. Very, very few street whores can do that. Very, very few pimps will even expect that. But, your child's mother, and the state, will fully expect that.

Continuing now, with that New York state of experience, you must begin to make payments immediately. This must continue until your place of employment receives an Income Withholding Order which directs them to deduct the payments from your salary. Remember that this order will include an arrears amount that is usually equal to half again of your ongoing payment. And remember that the child support amounts starts from the day that she files for it. Each time that you change jobs, you must do this. If you lose your job, you must go back to court and explain your new circumstances. You will still be responsible for the payments within the time lag that it takes to get a hearing.

If the amount of arrears are over $2,500.00,or over 4 months old, at any time during the next (up to)

21 years, you now become subject to the following sanctions.

A Lien against your property. If there is a problem with your arrears amount – and it does not matter how or why – you will receive, within 45 days in the mail after your last court date, a Intent to File a Lien notice. For those who might not know, a lien is a charge upon real or personal property for the satisfaction of some unpaid debt arising by an operation of law. Generally, a lien will block the sale of your house or car until that money that the lien represents is paid off. The notice warns that if you do not pay off the child support arrears plus the current child support within 35 days from the date of the notice, a lien for that amount will be placed upon your property – any property, not just a house or a car. Alternatively, you can mail an appeal, or prove that you do not owe so much, to the Office of Child Support Enforcement's own little kangaroo court. Please note that this kind of lien can apply to anything that you might own that has a perceived value. A search within the thicket of family court laws reveals that the state can issue a lien against anything you own, and assign a monetary value to it. So, your dear old Grandma's dinner plates in the kitchen can suddenly be worth $5,000.00. Your old Chevrolet Camaro, out rusting in the back yard, is now worth $10,000. And, how did the state find out about these possessions of yours? Well, your child's mother has previously sat down to an interview with the authorities, and told the state about everything that you value and hold dear to you. Yes, it is part of the process with the state for your child's mother to sit down with them and she gives up all she ever knew about you. There are other, even more intrusive services available to her as well.

Chances are, any attempt at a lien of that type will not go that far. But, in New York State, at least, the laws that permit that are on the books and the process does happen. Once a lien is filed, it might take hell and high water to get it off. The Notice of Intent to File is one of several shake downs that will be applied to you by the state.

Money Judgment. Within 30 days of your last day in court, if you are still behind in your arrears, the state will send to you a Special Notice that essentially says that the state will serve a Child Support Enforcement Execution Notice "upon the person in possession or custody" of the money belonging to you. This usually means that they can order your bank or credit union to empty your accounts. It does not matter to them if you have personal checks or automatic debits out there flying around. The bank or Credit Union can then charge you for bounced checks and administrative fees. And, how do they know which bank or credit union that you use? Well, your child's mother told them, of course. If you have received one of these notices that the state plans to go ahead with a "Child Support Enforcement Execution notice", then you had better move your money out of the bank to another safe place, such as a safe deposit box or even a shoebox under your bed. Again, the state will invite you to play their little game and send an appeal to their internal little kangaroo court. As an alternative, the state may deny your appeal but refrain from going ahead and serving that "Child Support Enforcement Execution notice". In this scenario, the state may hold this notice over your head in case the current child support payments are interrupted anytime in the future.

Tax Offset and/or Passport Denial. After 30 days, if you still have an arrears balance, the state will hit you with what is called a Tax Offset/Passport Denial. Although these are two separate actions, aimed at two different sets of fathers, both of these actions are handled by one office.

In either case, you are given 60 days from the date of the notice to either pay those arrears, along with the current child support bill, in full, or, once again, you can try to appeal their decision. If you do nothing, the state will "certify" any arrears amount that you might still owe at tax time later on this year, or the next year, or the year after that, and "intercept" or take any tax return monies due to you when you file your state or federal tax return, or both. It is important to keep on top of this particular sanction because the authorities will take your tax refund, even if it was jointly filed by you and your new spouse. There may be an "innocent spouse" defense for this.

As for the passport denial, well, this sanction is for those of you who have relatives in other countries, in case you are thinking of relocating. They may also feel that if you have enough money to travel, you might have enough money to pay for your child.

Driver's License Suspension. We will save the best, for last. About 15 days after your last court date, and, again, if you have those arrears, the state will send out to you a notice that will threaten to suspend your driver's license with 45 days of the date of the notice. You may be able to apply within the DMV for a restricted driver's license. Again, you must pay off the arrears or appeal this impending decision. Curiously, there is a third option here. You are invited to come in and make a "Satisfactory Payment Arrangement with us" for the amount of money in dispute. To do this, you might have to "Execute an Affidavit of Confession of Judgment" for the "total amount that you owe". This basically means that you have to rubber stamp and agree with the amount that they are looking for, even if their math is bad. A more apt description would be is for you to go there and lay upon your stomach on a table. After that, you would have to make the usual Satisfactory Payment Arrangement.

Chances are you might get all of these notices together, in one batch. Do not ignore these notices, even if you are presently unable to pay. You must reply, one way or the other, to these notices, as soon as you can. Try and handle this business. You might have to comply with the shakedown and empty out your savings, if any. Otherwise, things can get considerably worse. We won't even talk about the possibility of how you might end up in jail behind this.

What to do?

Well, what should one do in this situation? What if you are one of the unlucky 30% who just got hit with this judgment?

The actual child support amounts will take, in reality, roughly thirty to seventy percent of your after tax earnings. Like it or not, and I know it is all "not", you will have to downsize your life. You might have to lose that attractive black Mercedes or Lexus that you worked all that overtime for. That big new curved screen TV that the store says you can wait a year before making the first payment – well, you might have to tell the store to take it back. That weekly night out with the boys might have to become a monthly thing for the foreseeable future. You will have to sit down, and have to imagine your life on half of what you make. You will have to make really hard choices, and make hard decisions on what you can do without. And then, somehow, within the space of a couple of weeks, you will have to make it a reality. You will have to downsize, because it will not make any sense of having the normal financial pressure of the material things that you have next to the extreme financial pressure of a child support judgment. The child support judgment will become your new normal, up to eighteen or twenty-one years from now. The only thing that you should not consider getting rid of is a house. If you are over five years in on a mortgage, typically in most areas of the United States, a rented room may cost more. Additionally, you may be able to refinance or get a home equity loan in order to meet a financial pitfall, or emergency. You will not be able to do this if you are living in an apartment or a rented room. Avoid, at all costs, those places or people who specialize in lending to those who are in distress, such as a pawn shop or payday lender. This makes about as much sense as going to Dracula to stop the bleeding.

I am focusing on the financial part of this process because this is what you, the male, will have to focus on first. You will have to work upon your own finances before you do anything else. You will have to work upon you because no one else will. Most financial advisors will tell an adult to save for retirement and the adult's own well being before setting aside any money for the child's education. In this situation of child support, you will have to financially right yourself after having been "sunk" by the courts. And, by the way, do not expect the child's mother to set aside anything towards the child's education. In the American females' mind, that child support is "her" money, it is compensation, or even a paid wage, for having to raise the child. In her mind, all of the "heavy lifting", such as braces, a special class or even an education, is still your responsibility, over and above child support.

The reality is, basically, once you've started paying child support, you do not owe the mother anything else, period. The child support document may demand additional amounts for medical expenses and babysitting, and you will have to pay that, but you absolutely do not owe the mother anything else. If she took this road, let her walk it by herself. Now, depending upon your relationship with your child, it is up to you how much you feel that you can afford. It is up to you to see how much that you can save for the child's education. Do not sacrifice your future for that of the child. I don't give a shit how selfish that this sounds. Mister, you will have to understand that you will have to take care of yourself first, mainly because no one else will. Once you are separated from the family, most children won't even care about what happens to that dear old Dad who disappeared years ago. This is the naked truth. And, yes, it might seem selfish, but there are no lies within this book. You should, of course, be able to spend money upon the child whenever you can visit. But understand, that this is an expense separate and above that of child support. The money that you spend independently upon your own child will <u>NOT</u>, I said <u>NOT,</u> be counted as child support. ONLY what you pay to the state will be counted as child support. (And we still call this child support, not mothers' pimping money, or a pussy tax, or whatever).

Perhaps only your child will see that you cared, way back when. And, frankly, that is all you can wish for.

The Effects upon the Children Of Child Support

The effects upon the children when their parents separate is usually negative. When you look at it from the child's point of view, the child sees that his or her entire world is breaking up. The parents mean everything to them. Unfortunately, many divorces and breakups occur during the children's most formative years. This is exactly when the children need both parents the most, more than at any other time in their lives. The punitive nature of the child support process upon the father contributes mightily towards the children's worst fears. With the diminished presence, or even the absence of the father, the children may suffer the feelings of abandonment. And it is quite possible that the mother of the children might decide to help things along by alienating the children further ("See? He's not here. He doesn't care about you....").

The family court laws and the child support courts' effects upon the father usually serve to put the man into a financial tailspin from which it may take months or years to recover. Generally speaking, those families who were middle class or below suffer the most from this process. The children, who may miss the fathers' presence, may begin their own private tailspin from the emotional security of the family to the unknown emotional wilderness of the neighborhood. The seeds for later failure in life - such as failing grades in school - may have begun. The thing is that the children - if they are young enough - don't care about money. They are often oblivious to that part of the child support process. The young child yearns more for the presence of his father.

If there was a child support system that actually considers the emotional needs of the children first, we might be able to undo a lot of the mental baggage that the children are saddled with during the parents' breakup. But, again, the mental welfare of the child is not as important as the woman's need for money and control.

As time goes by, even with the child support being paid, and with the kids not seeing their father so much (maybe every other weekend), a kind of benign neglect sets in, even if the mother is not actively engaging in parental alienation. (Most of the time, she is, since most petitions for child support are filed in anger at the father). The father's influence will begin to wane, partly because other people (the teacher, the babysitter, and perhaps the new man) are crowded him out of the child's lives, and partly because of the father's new role as an "entertainer" for the children. The original father, during visitation, is more likely to spend time with the kids at the mall or at the movies, rather than giving his kids the direction that the children need.

This is not really the father's choice but there is little else for him to do, given the time restraints of visitation.

As even more time passes, as the children get older, they will see that the new coat and Christmas presents are coming from Mom, and not Dad, even if they know that he is paying for it somehow. So, Mom takes credit for everything, which makes life so much easier for her. She is secure in thinking that the children have been properly misled. Every now and then, she might throw in a ("Your father never cared for you anyway") for good measure. After some more time passes, most children will begin to dismiss the father from their lives without any more prodding from their mother.

With that, the mother's power play over the father over the souls of the children, is complete. She owes to the state a "debt of gratitude" for helping her to eventually force the father out of their children's lives.

TRUE CHILD SUPPORT

Listen, I realize that I have spent most of the preceding pages in this chapter telling you all about the real truths and negative effects of the current child support system --specifically, the New York State child support system.

However, that does not mean that I do not favor having a way or a system of supporting a child after the parents go their separate ways. The present, woman based child support system is not the answer. The present system, developed for women by women, mirrors and perpetuates a woman's hate and desire to punish a man who has left her by employing the power of the state against him. The present system's signature philosophy of dismissing the direct monetary contributions of the father after the mother files for support, and then forcing the father to pay the state, is all about usurping the father's place within the former household, and giving all the power to the mother. The effects of this power play against the father contributes mightily towards driving the father out of the familial picture, and it invites the mother to begin the process of parental alienation. At best, the emotional influence of the biological father is reduced to a fraction of what it once was. And most importantly, the emotional needs of the children, especially the male child, go unmet, and so he often starts down the road of juvenile delinquency, just like some children of single parents.

An alternative to the present system of hijacking the words 'child support' and substituting a mother's pimping service, would be to offer what I would call true child support. While I cannot be very specific, I would envision a system that would be something like what one does with an elder person who can be no longer responsible for his or herself. Perhaps there would be someone with a position that resembles that of a conservator who is hired out to oversee a certain number of child support agreements, or oversee the child support agreements from a certain area. Please notice, that I wrote the word "agreements". This means that there were two parents who agreed, or who were made to agree, how to proceed with their children past the point of their breakup. This also means that the same two parents have a plan in place for the support and care of their children. A provision should be made to save for the child's future college education. For a better sense of responsibility, both parents should actually pay into the child's money savings account. The custodial parent must be able to show, and justify those purchases made for the child that are over and above the child's simple and weekly needs. The parents should be able to meet on a monthly basis in front of the conservator and discuss these things. The conservator will have the power to enforce changes if the need arises. There may be those who might be better prepared to flesh out and elaborate on what I have proposed above.

I think that what I have proposed above – True Child Support – is a vast improvement over the present system. This way, the father is kept in the loop as far as the child is concerned. This way, visitation will be encouraged instead of discouraged. The child will benefit because the father will still be able to make some decisions about his or her life. The child will also benefit because this child support is actually for the child. Yes, the mother will lose some power, and she won't be able to spend indiscriminately. She will have to justify what she spends to the father and the conservator.

Unfortunately, I am confident in one thing. This will never ever happen. The very idea of changing the present system is anathema to the American woman at her core. It is also anathema to some lawyers as well. What I proposed above eliminates the American woman's God given (actually, law given) right to skewer and bleed her ex-husband or boyfriend. This also would eliminate the child as a pimping enabling object and a profit center. Also, some lawyers would have to do without an important profit center. For those reasons alone, the only place that you will ever see something like what I proposed above is right here in this book.

Please forgive me for being pessimistic about this. In the United States, women voters outnumber men, and women voters are more likely to get out and vote, especially when the issues at hand concern them. On Election Day, women are more likely to get out there and vote. Men are more likely to be quaffing a beer in a sports bar. Urp!

Remember, the present system is in place because the American woman as a group, want it that way.

SEXUAL HARASSMENT

Sexual Harassment

Now, perhaps we are getting into the outer rings within the American male-female interactive world. Sexual harassment is one of those totally subjective things that have the power to wreck a man's life or livelihood – on the judgment or word that a woman states to the authorities. Wikipedia defines sexual harassment as the "unwanted coercion or bullying of a sexual nature, or the unwelcome or inappropriate promise of rewards in exchange for sexual favors". A look at the Findlaw.com defines it as "employment discrimination consisting of unwelcome verbal or physical conduct directed at an employee because of his or her sex". These definitions seem pretty cut and dried. Perhaps only an ogre would defy those definitions above.

In real life, however, sexual harassment could be, in a woman's mind, a comment about her dress or hairstyle that may have been made one time too many. There are women out there – especially those from the younger (!) generation – who feel insulted and harassed from almost any compliment that you, the man, might give them. Some of these women have gone so far as to privately redefine whatever a compliment is to them, and who can give it. In their minds, only the men who are attractive to them may offer a compliment. These women are still enough of a minority that they can be dismissed as loons. Frankly, I, myself, will not compliment an American woman any more, no matter how she is dressed, or even naked, unless we are deeply into a conversation. You, mister, should do this as well. What you perceive as a compliment can now often be taken as harassment or a threat.

I used to think that the great majority of women actually took the time to seek out and enjoy most comments and compliments from men. Perhaps this is separate and apart from what nearly every woman seeks – to be noticed. To be noticed – silently, I guess – is what women will do while supporting the entire multibillion fashion and skin care and makeup industries. That's all for women, and their fervent wish to "be noticed".

Well, back to sexual harassment. You see, in my small opinion, there might be two different kinds of sexual harassment. There is sexual harassment on the job – which is stiffly defined above, by Wikipedia and Findlaw.com. And there is sexual harassment on the street, which may be defined however a woman on the street might choose to define it. The reality is, that a spoken word to a woman that you, the man thought was nice or clever, may devolve into a shouting match, or even an arrest from a nearby policeman.

The first, or "classic" kind of sexual harassment often begins within a working relationship with a female, or even within a group of females. What might be seen as mindless banter or talk by a male can be construed as harassment or negative innuendo by a female. ("if you're a good girl, I'll get you promoted"). Or sometimes, a touch might be deemed by her as inappropriate – even a touch on the shoulders, can also count, in a courtroom, as sexual harassment.

The sexual harassment charges that may result from what you, the man, thought was innocent flirting will turn out to be almost always fatal to your working career, mister. There really isn't a defense against whatever someone says, except for whatever you say, in your defense. I'm not trying to be slick with words here. For you, the man, during the "discovery" phase of a trial, everything that you said previously, even as a joke, will become suspect, and ripe for questioning. Very few men are able to stand up to that kind of scrutiny over any period of time. A charge of sexual harassment, even if it is not sustained, will leave mud all over your persona that you probably cannot remove. In addition, such a charge will stain your record, whether on paper or online. It will change what others think of you at your place of employment, and at subsequent places of employment. At a minimum, you could be looking at a prolonged period of unemployment.

To avoid such a situation, you, the male, must learn to modify your workplace conversations so that nothing can be construed as sexist or racist. In the office, keep your personal joking and humor to a minimum. Indeed, you should try and keep most of your conversations business related. If this makes for a boring and lifeless workplace, so be it. You can go ahead and imagine that the making an off-color comment about a controversial subject could result in a misconstrued perception of how you really are. The thing is, no one, except for a really close friend, will say anything to you about your verbal gaffe. But they will certainly discuss it with an investigator.

Yet, on the other hand, workplace romances do develop. The thing is, for you, the male, you must understand how things have changed. The things you might get away with saying outside your job might hang inside the office for years to come, if you broke up with her, and now she is contemplating a sexual harassment lawsuit. What you should do, mister, when a possible romance with a co-worker arises, is that you should hang back and let her make the first move. Mister, this is not negotiable. Let her be clear and unambiguous, let her make the sexual innuendo. I am not talking about being invited to make the first move, as most women will do. I am talking about inviting you out for coffee, or something of that nature. This way, if things go wrong, you could at least score points or whatever at a hearing or trial by saying that she made the first move. It all seems quite petty now, but it could be huge, later.

There's just one more thing to keep in mind. Sexual harassment seems to be mostly within the mind of the beholder. An exact line, where innocent flirting stops, and sexual harassment begins, has never been drawn. Even the most modest flirts can be turned into a monster's advances by a skilled lawyer in the courtroom. And, what it all boils down to, most of the time, is a he-said, she-said. And the only difference between winning and loosing is who said it better before a jury.

Torin Reid

My Own Experience

I could guess, that by now, dear reader, you might think that I must be some kind of bad actor, or a negativity magnet.

Somehow, I must have encountered and witnessed every negative thing that can happen between a man and a woman. Well, the above is not true. It was just twenty-five years of life, frequently populated by relationship nightmares that have prompted me to write this book. And many American men experience more than one episode of negativity with women. Like the rest of the human race, many men have just learned to bury things like this within their minds over time. Now, one might ask, what about the good things, the positive things that happen between men and women? My answer again, is that you do not need me to tell you about the good times. Indeed, you need to go out and experience them yourself rather than read about them in a book. My goal here is to warn you away from the possibility of the bad times.

With that said, I am now going to relate to you an episode in which a female co-worker tried to bring charges of sexual harassment against me. I never touched or verbally harassed this woman. Despite this, I consider myself to be extremely lucky to have kept my job. I was even able to recover, somewhat, from the assault of verbal mud that was thrown at

176

me. I am aware of the fact that normally, this does not happen. Indeed, what usually happens is that the man loses his livelihood and his reputation, no matter what the facts actually are.

Let me give you some background on this incident. It took place over a 90 day period back in 2008. At the time, I was working for the New York City subway as a train operator. I had already been with the subway for over twenty years at the time. For clarity's sake, let me explain to you that most New York City subway trains are run by a train operator, who drives the train, and a conductor, who opens and closes the doors and interacts with the trains' passengers. The train operator and conductor's jobs here are unionized and there is what is known as a "pick", or selection of runs based on one's seniority. The two job titles, taken together, are known as "crews", and they work together for about six months at a time, until the next "pick" or selection.

This is how it was with a female conductor that I was working with at that time. Despite the harassment allegations, I was forced to work with her during, and after the timing of this incident. These are my thoughts and feelings about this thing from that time.

Where do I begin with this? One would say, well, at the beginning. But there are several beginnings to this 90 day nightmare. Did it begin when she lived across the street from me? Here is where I learned a little bit about her, when rumor slowly began to turn into facts. I learned about how unstable she was as a person. She seemed to relish conflict. She had two children, and on visitation day, and the children's father had to pick up the children at the police station. I remember her telling that story to several people on the job with a tight little smile on her face. I paid no mind to this until we ended up working together on a subway line that, today, no longer exists. I had more seniority than she did; so I was the one who had picked the job first. When I found out that we would be working together, I decided to keep a little distance between us, rather than socialize with her.

Now, one might say, well, what is her side of the story? And, my answer is, to hell with that, this is my book. In here, she has no side of the story, although I will detail her actions. When today's young women decide to write their college rape stories, they do not decide to ask the men they accused for a say so in their books or magazine article. And, so it goes. Plus, when all this was going down, I effectively had no "side of the story". No one ever really asked, besides some immediate supervisors. No co-workers ever asked. They preferred to go along with the gossip. I had brought this incident to the union. The union's help was kind of lukewarm. Go and find that bitch if you really want her opinion.

So, anyway, we had begun working together in October, 2007. We did not speak much at first, except for work related conversations. Even so, our working relationship slowly began to deteriorate. As things began to get worse, I spoke less to her. I guess that I was supposed to notice that she was spending time and money going out and spending her money getting her hair done. Some of her hairstyles were pretty good, but I really did not feel so familiar to her enough to say anything. Our conversations, rare by now, ended when a few spoken words turned into a shouting match in the station, in front of other passengers. That experience was embarrassing and baffling; I was left wondering why she was like that. Needless to say, I decided to say nothing more to her. A few weeks later, there was a work day that had the inevitable subway delays. We were crawling along from station to station, so at several stations I had to signal her, using the trains' buzzer, to keep the doors open because we had to stay in the station longer than usual. As the slowly moving trains cleared up on the track ahead, I buzzed her again that she should close the doors so that our train could proceed. She then asked me over the trains' intercom system whether she should close the doors because the signal at the end of the station was yellow. I did not want to talk to her, and I thought that she should mind her business on moving the train. But I did not share those thoughts, and I merely told her "yes". I knew that the train ahead would soon move to a point ahead of me where that signal would turn green. This woman then hollered back that I was not the only one on this train and that I needed to be taught a lesson. I did not reply but I figured that this woman had finally gone off her rocker. Later that evening, at the end of the workday, I had prepared a statement of what had happened between us, and I had decided to take that statement in to work with me the next day. Normally, subway employees do not report on one another or write one another up, but her actions were not normal.

Imagine my surprise the next day when I reported for work, and I found the little office where I sign in to the job crowded with people who are normally not present. There were entirely far too many supervisors present. No one looked at me directly, so I naively assumed that I had nothing to do with what was going on. The superintendent of the subway line that I worked for at the time was present as well. She was a large, brooding woman who was leaning upon the countertop that was normally full of papers. She was looking at the door that I had just come through. Apparently, she was looking for the devil. Her stare was so intense, that I also looked at the closed door. To this day, I sometimes wonder what that person looked like in her mind.

However, another, lower level supervisor broke her reverie. "That's him", she said, in a not so subtle whisper. The superintendent wheeled around and focused her negative attention upon me. "What job do you work?" she asked. I was actually startled by her simple question. She had spoken in a conversational voice, yet she seemed to have some anger behind it. When I finally began to answer her, she dismissed me with "Nevermind. I'll find out later." Only now did it begin to dawn on me that something was very, very wrong. I was glad that I had taken the time yesterday to write that statement. At that moment, I thought that all of this activity was overkill. I still had no idea that I was being accused of sexual harassment. But, just then, the female conductor that I was working with yesterday stepped out of an adjoining office. A couple of supervisors were with her. Once again, she had that evil, tight little smile across her face. A male supervisor followed close behind her. He reassured her, saying "don't worry, we'll do everything we can to protect you." I struggled to comprehend that. The conductor walked right by me, apparently feeling a victory that I still had no idea about. The female superintendent got my attention once more. "You'll have to write a statement" she said. I gave her the paperwork that I had. She seemed surprised that I had already done this.

While I was in the train during the workday, my mind was reeling. This is most certainly not the time to lose one's attention to the tracks ahead but I could not put what happened earlier that day out of my mind. I drove the train like a robot, basically by reflex. At the terminals, I looked right through my conductor, not saying anything. At the scheduled lunch hour in the crew room on the job, I felt that there was a subtle change in there. Normally, in the crew room, I keep pretty much to myself, but I will speak with those who are around me. But on this day, I could not put my finger on it, so to speak. I guess you can call me slow or naive or stupid but I did not think that the rumor or gossip could possibly travel that fast. I did notice that none of the "in" people – actually, the biggest gossips – did not deign to even say "hi". I figured that I would know what was going on by the end of the workday.

And, I did. On the last trip of the day, three – yes, three supervisors were riding the train. None of them made themselves known until the last four or five stops. One supervisor, a female, asked me straight out, "What happened?" I told her about the previous day's altercation, and she seemed confused. Perhaps she thought that I was lying. At the terminal, a male supervisor asked the same thing. "What happened?" he said. Again, I related what had happened the previous day. He thought that I was lying, as well.

I finally got the "big picture" when a male superintendent pulled me aside. He stated that my conductor had filed a harassment case against me. He did not use the word "sexual", but he said that she had stated that I was harassing her, that I would not leave her alone, and that I wanted to "take her over" and be her man. I only hoped that my speechless face reflected my surprise to him. The superintendent continued by saying that he had to write it up and then send it downtown – and then he finished with "that's it" – meaning that I would no longer have a job. He then turned and left, leaving me open jawed at the top of a set of stairs at the terminal station.

I could not believe what I was hearing. I might as well had been hit in the head with a baseball bat or something. I felt that woozy. I tried to flip the pages within my head, and figure out what the hell could have happened to cause this. After spending some time, standing there and doing this, I came up blank. I never touched her. I never even shouted at her. Indeed, this woman had verbally abused me. I signed out of the job for the day, and went straight home. Getting any sleep that night was out of the question, so I ended up spending the night online. Presumably, I was thinking that someone else had gone through something like this, and might now be able to give advice. There was one such person, but you had to go to his website and pay for the content. Other web pages were nothing but long winded ads for lawyers. That was not what I needed that night. There was very little advice for anyone who had just been accused of sexual harassment. Coming to this frustrating conclusion took most of the night, and I decided to call in sick the next day. I take my job seriously, and I try not to go in to work when I know that I will be tired or sleepy. Later on that afternoon, after I awoke, the weight of the accusation hit me again. How in the hell was I going to live if I did not have this job? I was (and I still am) living paycheck to paycheck. I thought about another guy on the job who was fired for sexual harassment, after he had bought a married (!) woman a washing machine and a dryer. How that situation came to be, I still don't know, but that guy lost 12 or 13 years towards a pension. After awhile, I realized that I had to get this nonsense out of my head, and get some real answers. I spent the rest of this day seeking help. A call to the union yielded a very sympathetic female union official, someone who was a friend before this day. She told me to gather all of my information and send it over to her. This was happening on a Friday, and it took a large part of the weekend to lay out my thoughts and prepare a package for her. You have already read some of what I wrote back then. Still, I was not sure that the union's efforts would be enough. I became convinced that I had to spend thousands of dollars, from I don't know where, and a couple of years, maybe, to clear my name. Then, I went out and got a copy of the Chief-Leader newspaper. This newspaper covers New York City and the surrounding area and it serves the city and state civil service employees. Within this newspaper, I was able to find two lawyers who claimed to represent those who might find themselves in trouble within the civil service environment. Neither one sounded particularly interested in my case when I called them. One of them even said "Well, most of you guys are guilty, anyway". Hmm. And I would want this guy to defend me in court? The other lawyer told me that I had the right to request information from the other side, or at least those people who were representing her. Then I should get back to him. This nugget of information gave me, at least, a task to do once I returned to work on Monday. For once, the weekend passed slowly, in part because I stayed home and worked on the paperwork I needed for the union. I also told a few of my incredulous male friends about what had happened. Of course, I told none of my female friends.

Monday came. Before going to work, I had to fax to the union my statements on the situation. Again, the friendly female official promised me that she would get this to the right people so that a defense may be prepared. Later on that day, I reported for work and saw my name on the sign on sheet. Seeing my name there told me that, at least for now, I still had a job. At the beginning of the day, several coworkers with whom I thought were at least a nodding acquaintance with no longer spoke or even nodded. Later on, I told my immediate supervisor, who was by now omnipresent, that I had the right to request information on what was being said about me and what charges were being prepared. During lunchtime, I met with so other coworkers who knew me a little better than the others did, and so I laid out everything to them. I knew, up to that point, that I still had to work with the person who accused me of sexual harassment, and now it was war, on every level. I even told them what I knew about her before this happened. Most of them were quite surprised (or maybe faked being surprised) that this would happen to me, and not to some other persons who were far more forward than I was, and who had made reputations for themselves. A couple of others shared some lurid tales of other men who were victims of sexual harassment accusers. Those tales left me with a sinking feeling. In no case did the male in any of these stories prevail. Some guys did survive these accusations, but no man was able to rise above the mud and loss of reputation.

During this working day, I had said nothing to my accuser. At one end of the subway line, the trains went further below ground, down yet another level, so that they may reverse direction and head back downtown for another trip. The normal procedure was for the train operator to advance the train to a certain marked point, stop the train there, and then walk through the train to the last car, which now becomes the first car. In this process he or she walks past the conductor who normally sits in the middle of the train. While doing this, I would have to face my accuser in this manner three times every workday. Luckily for me, she was no longer on the train at least for the first few weeks. Perhaps she has convinced someone that I would exact revenge down there.

A few days later, I called the union to check on the progress of my paperwork. The friendly female union official told me that she had read and forwarded my paperwork to another, higher placed union official, and that I should contact him from now on. I did so, and I reached him after several tries. He also said that I would have to wait for a statement or paperwork from the other side so that a hearing may be scheduled. Later on the same day, I also heard back from that immediate supervisor. He said to me that the answer to my request for information was "no". With that answer, I could not really call back that lawyer that I had the short conversation with. At least, that is what I had thought at the time. And that was where the whole thing sat, for days and days. No one in authority spoke to me, about anything, but I knew that they were around. All of my coworkers around me knew about me and what was going on, but no one spoke anymore on that subject. Most of the men were silently sympathetic, but they fully expected me to disappear one day and so they kind of disassociated themselves from me. The feeling was kind of like when animals run together in a herd, and then one animal drops out from exhaustion or pain or whatever. The other animals in the herd might have been sympathetic, but they were not about to stop running. Curiously, most of the female coworkers were not hostile to me. There were a couple who turned their faces away but they were friends of the accuser. I sensed something less than hostility from most others. And a couple more spoke, and even flirted with me. But I was having none of it. For me, all female coworkers were suspect. My social world became very small. Some days, I did not speak to anyone.

After perhaps three weeks, my accuser lost her privilege of not having to ride the train far underground with me. Therefore, in order to avoid her, I had to dismount from the train that I was driving, and walk alongside of it to the opposite end, upon adjacent active tracks. I was very careful while dodging the other trains, but I sure did not need that added element of danger to the workday. But when it all came down to either dodging the trains, or risking another incident with someone that I thought was unstable, I thought that it would be better to dodge the trains. The trains, at least, stayed on their rails. The trouble was, that all of this climbing down, and walking around took time away from our break time and the lunch time as well. Other crews would see me on the tracks and they would ask why later on. Once the word got around, the subway terminal switching tower routed my train even further back, towards the end of the underground relay tracks, making my journey somewhat safer, but at the expense of more break and lunch time. My accuser hated all of this and so I drew a little satisfaction out of that.

There was no use complaining about what was going on. In fact, I began to sense that a majority of the people around me did not believe, or at least had serious doubts, about me being a sexual harasser. At the other end of the line downtown, I told those in charge there about my situation. Soon, my accuser found it best to simply stay on the train at that end of the line.

Still, the lack of any official action, either for or against me, was driving me nuts. I had to be hyper careful every day. There was a fairly long list of people who I had learned to avoid, or simply not even look at, starting with my accuser, with whom I was still working with every day. Someone had suggested to me that I should go to the union and change over to another run but I was not going to do that, since that would make me look even worse. Within the subway system, they have thirty working days, or actually six weeks to bring formal charges or start a proceeding against you. After about four weeks of not knowing what was going to happen, I was ready to make something happen. Another call to the union got me put on hold, forever. I was never able to reach them after that time. And after that, I wrote a letter to the president of the subway system detailing my situation, and what was (not) presently going on. I wrote similar letters to the general superintendent and some other bigwigs. Surprisingly, only the president of the subway system replied. He directed me to get in contact with the agency's director of equal opportunity and employment. When I finally met this man, he was evasive, and he would not enlighten me on anything despite having a two inch stack of papers on display at a conference table. When I asked him what the papers were about, he became even more evasive, and then he hid them away. I ended up being pretty angry with this guy – I told him that I knew I was innocent, dammit! (Without knowing how to prove this). I ended up leaving that meeting more baffled than when I came in.

The first real inkling that there was a light at the end of this particular tunnel was when another supervisor took it upon himself to take the long walk down to the lower level tracks to meet my train. After he met me there, he told me to stop writing letters, and I believe that he said to "just let everything go." Without waiting for an answer, he then turned and disappeared into the subterranean darkness. My reaction to that was what was I trying to hold on to? It was them – meaning my accuser, and the subway system's local leadership in general, that was trying to get rid of me. My second reaction was that this man was one of the most trustworthy persons in the system, supervisor or not, so what he was saying had to carry some weight. But, there were at least two more weeks under the sword of Damocles. And, even after the subway system's management was no longer able to bring charges, I still had to work with my accuser.

The two weeks passed by, without incident. I stopped walking around the outside of my train at the end of the run. But I still had to face my accuser each time that I had to walk back through the train. I hope that she saw a man who was stony faced and silent.

Our "pick", or job would end in about a month or so. I had already chosen greener pastures out on another line. It took some doing, but I completed most of those weeks much as I did during the time when I had to worry about being charged. One day, I thought that it was bizarre, when my accuser asked why I was not speaking to her. I replied that I had nothing to say to her. Then, she was upset all over again. And, about another week later, I had gotten a second "inkling" about what had happened downtown. Again, in a darkened spot within the subway station this time, another supervisor whispered to me that "there was no sexual harassment". I was incredulous that this verdict was known to everyone except me. Apparently, the "paperwork" had gone "downtown", but someone who had seen these things before had determined that this harassment was all her fantasy. The area supervisors had apparently also been told, or decided not to speak to me on this subject. But a couple of them took some time out, despite the danger of a reprimand, or worse, to speak to me.

And, my accuser? Well, as far as I know, nothing ever happened to her. She had begun acting as if nothing ever happened, as well. On the next to the last week before the pick ended, she even found the time to say "goodbye". I definitely gave her a "goodbye" as well. She was on vacation the following week.

As a postscript, after I had moved on to another line, a fellow coworker called me. He said that when the some of the other workers within the old crew room saw that I was no longer there, one guy said that I was sent to a "program" of some sort. I reassured my caller that I was not in a program but that I was working on another line. I have not been back there since that time. My accuser continued to work the same job as before. I told the new train operator who now worked with her what had happened. He felt that he would have no problems with her. But it really pissed me off that nothing ever happened to her – not even a reprimand – for concocting a lie, threatening my livelihood, and making all of the supervisors run crazy. And, the lawyer? Well, he said. Nothing punitive ever really happened to you, so you really have nothing to sue for. What about my fried brains, and not knowing whether I had a job for six weeks, and having to work with her? Well, his reply pretty much added up to "be a man, suck it up".

In closing, I don't blame the subway supervisors for doing what they did. They had no idea, at least in the beginning, what really happened. (And, neither did I!). I had lived, and worked through the longest three months of my working life. But, as I write this, six years after it happened, I still get angry at that woman, who apparently is living and working, free to fuck up another man's life.

What to do about Sexual Harassment?

When I was writing the previous essay on what was a false allegation of sexual harassment against me, I recalled all of the same surprise, anger, loathing, and most of all, utter helplessness as I wrote those 90 plus days in my life not so long ago. Looking back, I still feel that it was only through the luck of the draw, and the sharp eye of some unknown legal analyst, that I was able to keep my job. As far as I can tell, this person looked at what she wrote and saw the holes in her story. I know, in my heart, that I did not harass or touch that woman. I also know that what I know in my heart might not be enough to defend me at a trial or a hearing. When I think of what I had heard about other sexual harassment cases, apparently all that it takes for the man to lose is a judge or a hearing officer that would have been less than objective; or one who is sympathetic to the female.

Even worse, there really is no hard and fast line beyond which a man should not go. Sexual harassment is up to the discretion – or the level of disgust – of the person that it is directed to. One person's sassy flirt is another person's disgusting remark. With that in mind, I really do not see a positive way out of a sexual harassment allegation, whether you, the male, are innocent or not. Even if you beat the formal charges, you may not be able to wash off all of the mental and social mud that comes with such an allegation. Take a moment and try to imagine being, for example, a supervisor of both men and women within an office environment. Imagine trying to inspire your "team" to perform beyond the company's expectations. Every word that you say would be hyper-analyzed, with multiple opinions. Some of your subordinates would wonder why the company stuck you upon them. It would be a mistake to even talk to any woman on your team alone. Imagine that you might forget yourself and say, "Hey, you have to take one for the boys, ok?" I guess I am being a little ham-handed on that last one, of course. But it is easy to see how your effectiveness, in any position, would be compromised after a sexual harassment allegation. Within the corporate environment, losing your job might be part of any settlement. With what I've described above, losing your job might be a relief.

Perhaps the best defense might be your reputation within the work place before the accusation was made. Perhaps you may be able to find enough co-workers who are willing to testify in your behalf. If so, you might be able to knock down or ameliorate the charges before you.

If you find yourself as the victim of sexual harassment, this may be a real uphill battle. After all, how many people are going to believe that a female supervisor or a homosexual male supervisor made your workplace so intolerable because of a few spoken phrases? You will have to go beyond that, and be ready to prove a real degradation of the work environment, such as false performance reports and the like.

I wish that I could offer a better outlook on this subject. However, I have not heard of anything - certainly not a change in the laws - that would signal a change for men since the incident which I was a part of several years ago.

DOMESTIC VIOLENCE

DOMESTIC VIOLENCE

Within this book of sometimes thorny issues, perhaps it is the subject of domestic violence that is the thorniest prong in the entire relationship rose bush. There are more lies and prejudgments here than in most of the other subjects discussed by this book.

Why is this? There are many reasons. One of the main reasons is that domestic violence has been one of the most egregious and personal means of control of one person by another. This is usually, but definitely not always defined as the male controlling the female by using violence or the threat of violence.

Women who choose to stay (and, yes, this is often a choice, despite what the female advocates say) often stand the chance of being hurt or killed by their mates (not just men) during a bout of domestic violence. At the height of an argument, men also stand the chance of being hurt or killed this way, but this does not happen as often, and far fewer people seem to care. Both men and women believe that a woman's hand won't hurt anybody – until that hand is holding a knife or a gun. By then, it is too late.

Believe it or not, men also suffer from domestic violence, or, better put, domestic abuse. It is women, more than men, who seek to control the relationship. Sometimes, a woman may become bored with the relationship, or they realize that they have "settled" as they call a man who they feel is beneath them. These women often become verbally abusive, and they never miss an opportunity to denigrate and downgrade him. Sometimes this type of woman is simply a nag who thrives on a negative relationship with her husband or spouse. This negative relationship is also a kind of control that a woman imposes upon a man. This is most likely to occur when a man loses his job, or takes a demotion, or somehow in some way, his status as "a man" or provider, is reduced. This too, is domestic abuse. Men who have become used to this kind of abuse need to get themselves to a safe mental place, such as a friend or relative's house, if only for a daily or even a weekend visit. Once there, then perhaps these men can find some sort of mental equilibrium, and make themselves better able to deal with their abusive wives or girlfriends.

The thing is, that kind of verbal (and sometimes physical) abuse suffered by men is never really addressed by the state. Nor is any of the infrastructure set up the state that is normally used to help the woman. Therefore, the police and the courts will never really understand how she baited you by calling you names, or saying things such as "hit me! I dare you!" Yet, this is the most prevalent type of abuse that is suffered by men. The court will only recognize that, hey, you finally did hit her. There are no safe houses or shelters for men. After all, a man can take care of himself, right? And most men would be too embarrassed to show up at such a place anyway.

A man in an abusive relationship has to find it within himself to effect a change within his relationship on his own, without any help.

Of course, things are 180 degrees different for women. There are stereotypes and built in prejudgments that are very hard, if not impossible, to alter. The overwhelming view of American society is the negative stereotype of a unibrowed Neanderthal, or maybe just a punk, who flies off the handle at the slightest provocation, and beat up a long suffering and defenseless woman. Now, most American men see themselves as anything but a Neanderthal or a punk. Most men see themselves as chivalrous and fair, especially to the opposite sex. Most men will say that they would never, ever, hit a woman, no matter what. Maybe even if he caught her having sex with somebody.

Well, what is generally not known is that these punks and Neanderthals, who are often called "batterers" (what a violent epithet) actually constitute but a small fraction of total relationships, period. Most relationships that are tagged as domestically violent are regular couples who have argued, or maybe even have gotten into a fight. Such a fight may have gotten out of hand, in the view of a neighbor, who then may have had called to police. I would say that a typical couple's fight would have involved both of them fighting, rather than the one sided attack of a "batterer".

In a survey conducted by the Family Research Laboratory at the University of New Hampshire, they found that men were the sole abusers in 10 percent of the relationships. Women were the abusers in 21 percent of the relationships. Yes, you read that right. Woman were the abusers in 21 percent of the relationships. Both partners were the abusers (of each other) in 69 percent of the relationships that were sampled by the university. This information appeared in the New York Daily news, and in other newspapers, on May 24, 2006. This article was buried way inside the paper. And Yes, I know that this information is dated. Perhaps that was the last time that somebody told the truth. But are you beginning to get enlightened, mister?

Where you stand, legally

Let us go back to that stereotypical Neanderthal who habitually beats up his long suffering wife that I wrote about in the previous essay. I will repeat that most men see themselves as being anyone but that "type" of person. Again, most men would never hit a woman. I'm even sure that someone will tell me not to compare such a man (that would hit a woman) to Neanderthals. After all, the Neanderthals were early hunter-gatherers long before the arrival of the present man.

However, what you really need to know, as a modern male human being, is that, legally, there is no difference between you, a man who might have had an argument with his wife or girlfriend, and that domestic violence Neanderthal. If the police show up at your door, in their eyes, there is no legal difference between you and that "punk". In the courtroom, there is no difference between you and that "batterer". You will be seen as that "type" of guy, and you will have little or no opportunity to explain yourself.

Indeed, if the police actually do show up at your door, you can add in to this volatile mix a heavy dose of the policemans' own prejudgments, and a sharply higher chance of you – the male – being hurt or killed. Just imagine your wife or girlfriend, in her anger at you, letting the police into your house, and she is shouting to them that you have a knife or a gun. Yes, things could end very badly for you, and you would know why.

Again, if and when you are in front of a judge, the only difference between you and that "batterer" who has been to court five times, is four arrests. Furthermore, it is quite possible for you to be put out of your own house or apartment that very night – and no one cares if you have money for a hotel. Later on, in the courtroom, should things get that far, you could be barred from you own home on an extended basis or be served a restraining order that severs all contact between you and your wife or girlfriend. Think about this – all of this will grow out of a few words that she said to the police.

I hope that you guys are picking up what I'm putting down here. It is as easy as hell to get into this kind of trouble, especially if you have a wife or girlfriend with a volatile personality. Listen, fellas, if you do not have a relationship that is serene as the beach at sunset, this is something that you have to watch out for, and keep in the back of your mind. In fact, you should insist that your relationships be as serene as the beach at sunset, or whatever scene that you might imagine.

With a domestic violence complaint against you, the slide downward is especially steep. I know that there are some of you who do not believe me, or think that this will never ever happen to you, because you are not that "type" of guy. And then there are those who could not care less about a restraining order. But I will counter with the fact that it is much better to read and find out about these things now, when you are reading this book, and not later, when a gruff police officer is explaining this to you.

And let me say this again, for the non-believers, and the "regular guys" above, that it is far easier than you think, to get stamped with that scarlet letter of being a domestic violence perpetrator. And the rest of you guys can pay attention to the next few paragraphs, as well.

The following is from a thick flyer that is offered to women by the New York State Office of Temporary and Disability Insurance. The flyer tells women that they are able to – and should – call a domestic violence hotline if the following relationship problems occur. Check out these six questions:

1). Is the other person (the man, of course) "Making you afraid?"

2). Is the other person stalking, or checking up on you, or following you?

3). Is the other person constantly putting you down, or telling you that you are worthless?

4). Is the other person threatening to hurt you, your children, or someone close to you?

5). Is the other person forcing you to have sex when you don't want to, or to do sexual things that you don't want to?

6). Is the other person physically hurting you, for example, by pushing, grabbing, slapping, hitting, choking, or kicking you?

Take a minute, and read these guidelines again. Chances are that you, or your wife or girlfriend, have been in at least one of the above scenarios, especially if you've been together for a long, long time. Numbers one through four could have occurred during a bad patch in any relationship. Number five could be taken as rape. Don't ever get involved with that. Number six, I believe, is more likely to happen to the man. And number three is also more likely to happen to the man. Lose your job, and you will find that out. And, good luck calling a domestic violence hotline as a man, reporting against a woman.

In any case, if numbers 1, 3, 5, and 6 are ongoing in your relationship, then you, the man, need to make plans to leave this relationship immediately.

Remember, these guidelines are given to women who are contemplating having you arrested and removed from your domicile. In my opinion these "standards" are set fairly low, from a domestic and a legal point of view. An argument or blowup – just one argument or blowup – could result in a breach of these guidelines. And, conceivably, that one breach could land you in jail. And if that does not land you in jail, here are some more questions that are far more likely to put you there. In October 2014, the New York City Police Department came out with a new policy that requires domestic violence victims (the woman) to answer six questions so that they are better able to go out and arrest the husband or boyfriend. Note that the questions are gender specific. This is why I put "the woman" in parenthesis. The six questions are:

1). Where does he work?

2). What kind of car does he drive?

3). Where does he hang out?

4). Where do his family or friends live?

5). Is he on social media?

6). Where should the police look for him?

The NYPD's goal, as stated in an October 4, 2014, New York Daily News article is for the NYPD to catch the man as soon as possible after the alleged crime. In the article, the police state that they are mindful of the fact that many women change their minds about going through with a prosecution of their husbands or boyfriends after the initial arrest. By getting the answers to those six questions, the public spokesman crowed, "We can investigate and prosecute even if the victim does not cooperate".

This "get 'em while he's hot" approach differs markedly form other sets of questions that are now posed to domestic violence victims in other police departments across the country. Elsewhere, domestic violence advocates and police departments ask alleged domestic violence victims a series of questions, such as "Did he say that he was going to kill you?", in order to determine the level of danger that the alleged victim actually faces. If that person is found to be in extreme danger, only then are all the stops pulled out to find and arrest the perpetrator. The NYPD, in contrast, apparently shares the feminist view that men must be made permanently wrong, in the first instance. Imagine the police arresting you at work or posting "You're gonna get arrested" on Facebook.

It would be a great idea if you, the male, or better yet, all men, would insist upon having a few rules of their own. We can start by telling a woman that if the policeman enters the home, the relationship will be over. I say this because, again, the level of danger for you, the man, rises markedly when a policeman enters your home. Tell her that the relationship will be over, and mean it. Seriously, the police expect the worst during a domestic violence call, and their worst will be directed at you. Mister, this could be a smart, pre-emptive move for you.

Taken together, the domestic violence flyer, and the police questions, can act as a virtual invitation for a woman to entrap and destroy any man that they get mad at. Make no mistake about this. The American woman absolutely loves it when she can fall back and play the victim, and simply watches while society, in the form of the police and the courts, goes about doing her bidding. These guidelines and questions are all about making men wrong, and putting them in jail, rather than solving a problem that resulted in an argument or domestic violence.

ARE YOU IN A VOLATILE RELATIONSHIP?

Hopefully, I've given you something to think about in the previous essays in this chapter. Here, I would like to bring to light yet another facet of this domestic violence problem. But first, Mister, perhaps you should take a moment to think about, and give some thought to, your present relationship. If you don't see a path forward, then you should think about ending the relationship. Think of all the things that you might have at risk, just by continuing to be in such a relationship, such as a damaged future, loss of your possessions, and maybe your freedom. If you need to exit this relationship, exit it standing up. You may lose money and possessions, but the eventual peace of mind you will have is priceless.

Let's put a fork in the road here. Ask yourself (we don't need her for this) about the real, and present status and your position in this relationship. Be as forthright and objective as you can, because your future depends on it. Listen – do you think your relationship is going down in flames? Have the police been called to your door? Have they just "dropped by", just in case? The police showing up at the front door should be cause for ending the relationship right there on the spot. If this is the case, you may want to skip over to the next essay in this chapter. You might be facing a brewing personal emergency.

Sometimes, a volatile relationship (and by this, I mean a relationship where there is constant arguing and fighting) is merely the symptom of a deeper problem within the relationship, such as money, or the lack of money. Needless to say, the solution would be to get to the bottom of the money problem. And yes, I know that this is easier said than done.

Often, the reason for a volatile relationship lies with the woman. She might have been so psychologically damaged, prior to meeting you, that she might actually enjoy the arguments and fighting. Some women conduct an affair this way, by starting an argument, and storming out of the house for a few hours, or a few days. Or maybe, she might enjoy stretching the relationship to the breaking point, just to see if she can get away with it. Or, it could be just a matter of control. Many women feel that they have to control the relationship, and making you angry is, to them, just another test. To these women, it's just like turning up the fire on the stove to high – useful if she wants a cup of coffee. And then there are those women who just must have attention, whether it is negative (an argument) or positive (lovemaking), and everything in between. For these women, the absolute worst thing for them is inattention (ignoring her). This might be a good way to punish her.

If you feel that things are a little bumpy but the relationship itself might be saved, well, you will have to take yet more time for yourself and think it through. To try and find the real problem, you've got to take a far closer look at your woman than you have before, even past those possibilities that I have mentioned above. Yes, I've said this previously, in other chapters. But, you are in a problem relationship now, and you need to hear this again, well, I'm saying this again. Look at what she does, and why she does it. What makes her tick? Does she actually do any of the possibilities that I have mentioned (damaged, affair, control freak?) Why is she this way? And, uh, take note, she has analyzed you in this fashion, with her friends, a long time ago.

Keep in mind, that most people (men and women) cannot really change who they basically are. Sometimes, women pretend to be different from who they really are, just so that they can get married. They put up an act so that they can trap the unsuspecting man. Perhaps a woman can change, with an extended bout of psychotherapy – but will they do this for a husband or boyfriend? Probably not – since women will make changes to themselves after the relation is dissolved, of course. There's one more thing to consider. Maybe it's you who needs to change? Just a thought. But if you cannot live with her as she currently is, it may be time to leave her. Only you can be the judge of this.

Personally, I don't see having to put up with a life with someone that is less than steadfast and nurturing. Some women may not even know how to be positive within a relationship. What are you willing to put up with? Yet another argument? Once a month? Once a week? Daily?

If you can talk with her, try to sit her down and get to the truth of the matter. She where she stands, and explain your position. Try your best to listen to and understand her position as well. If you do not understand her position, tell her so, and make her make you understand. So much can be avoided if the two of you can work this out.

With all of the above – all of it – keep in mind that your position remains legally precarious, no matter how calm and centered you are. Think about it – whenever an argument gets out of hand, or if you go "out of control", or appear to be a threat, she always has the choice to call the police, and have you taken care of so that she wins and you lose.

What is your choice if and when she goes "out of control?" Well, you can call the police. Maybe they might arrest her. Maybe not. What is most likely to happen is that when the police arrive, this sets off a "roulette wheel" of several possible outcomes, one of which includes you, the man, getting arrested as well. The arriving police may not believe that a woman can initiate domestic violence. Or maybe your wife of girlfriend is a great liar. (See, I told you that you should watch her more closely).

Now, let's go to the other side. What if the violence actually does come from you? I'm not talking about being defensive, or even being mad. (But you should be aware that making you angry may be a part of her plan). I'm talking about the kind of anger that makes you enjoy smacking that bitch. I'm talking about the kind of anger that wells up in you, and makes you explode, just like those Neanderthals that the authorities say that everyone is. I mean, what if you can't help yourself? What if your need to argue your point, or whatever it is seems to be is uncontrollable? If this happens to you, use that last, faint sliver of rational mind that is left, you know, that voice that says "Don't do this", and turn around and leave the house. Right now. In mid-sentence. Don't take time to explain. Go to your car, a park, even a bar. Once there, try to turn the situation over. Look at it from another angle, if you can. One thing is certain – anger and violence will not solve the problem. At the same time, I'm not saying that you are not entitled to be violent. There is no one telling women not to be violent, I'm not going to tell you not to be violent. But, I'll say again that anger and violence will not solve the problem. Even if you catch her in the act of screwing another man, violence, if justified, will only make things worse. Your ego will eventually survive the bruising. There are plenty of guys sitting up in prison, wishing that they had not wielded that baseball bat or pulled that trigger. They wish that they did not continue to choke her. Listen, I know that plenty of men fantasize about killing that bitch. But, let's go for a minute outside of your anger and your ego. Think ahead. Think about the child who would forever miss his mother. That same child will grow up fantasizing about killing you. And if she does not have children, think about her family members. Imagine facing a brother or sister of hers, gun in hand, and bent on revenge. Imagine trying to flip the pages in your head so that you can come up with the right words to make them put that gun down.

After all this, if you still cannot reconcile, and or restrain your anger, please try and seek some help, from a (preferably) male counselor or psychiatrist. I'm not saying you're crazy – yet – but you need to hear another point of view, or another comment on your potentially damaging behavior, from someone who is best suited to understand you.

In addition, you should think of this as well. The current justice system is set up for men to go down the drain into prison. After all, once a woman considers you to be unfit and worthless (at least emotionally) to her, the court system (especially the Family Court) is not unlike a garbage disposal, where the goal is to remove you from her and shake out your net worth. The woman and the courts expect you to be angry and violent – they are set up for that – and defeating the system by not falling into its well-greased traps will be a solid win for you.

And one more thing. Don't hold that anger in. Try and discharge your anger in a positive manner. Finish those projects. Work overtime – or even another job. Change your social circle. It might all work out for the better.

So, what do you do?

I will not waste your time here. What follows will be some suggestions and ideas about what you, as a man, should do about domestic violence, of basically, any long running feud or problem with your wife or live in girlfriend. If you find yourself in an argument or fight, and it is escalating, AND you are not yet (!) injured, you should leave immediately and find a safe place to recover your mind. While you are at this safe, but temporary place, you should make plans to leave this relationship as soon as possible. I guarantee you, that you will not like it if she makes plans for you to leave this relationship, via the police, and courts, etc. Keep in mind that this breakup may be exactly what she wants.

Now, it might be that you do not have any other place to live, at least not right now. In this case, you must minimize any and all chances for intimate contact. (You're not still sleeping with her, are you?). Listen to me. Get the hell out of the bedroom. Sleep on the couch. Take over another room, even if it was the living room. Establish another spot in the residence to call your own. Wall it off or at least hang a sheet over it. Yes, this might look silly, but if she does call the police, you can point out, with evidence, that you have tried to de-escalate the situation by keeping yourself apart from her. Let the police see this. Let them see your "tent" or whatever you might erect inside the house. More importantly, let the court see this. Take some pictures of your "tent". And I mean real, printable pictures, not just some cellphone snapshots. You must be able to show these pictures to a lawyer or a judge. This is particularly important, because, in many states, leaving the shared home can become grounds for abandonment in a divorce.

And, should you find it necessary, don't stop there. Skip meals if you have to, and other times that you and your spouse are normally together. If there are children around, take the time to explain to them that Daddy can't really be around Mommy right now, and that you hope that the problem will be resolved soon. If simple communication becomes a problem with her, then, make her text you. This creates a record. Yes, all these things might seem to be at the apex of silliness while you are sitting here and reading this book, and all is well. Don't worry, because if things go wrong, all of this stuff will become quite relevant.

If you do have somewhere to go, go there, so that you can minimize the chances for a confrontation. But leave your new, tented "bedroom" intact, so that it cannot be said that you have left the home completely.

And Other Consequences

In previous essays, I would like to think that I have covered all 360 degrees in the domestic violence spectrum, at least from a man's point of view. But let us take one more spin around this subject, because as men, we need to consider this.

We need to try and think ahead and not be reactionary. It is better, far better to sit down and form a plan of action to get yourself out of this relationship. It might even be better to form a plan of non-action or non-engagement; more on that in the next essay. Remember, if you don't have a plan, the consequences can get rapidly worse. Think ahead, mister, and think about this. Once you are tarred with the scarlet letter of being a domestic violence perpetrator, you will be marked for most of your life. It does not matter what really happened, or how you were convicted. The average person's reaction to a person with a domestic violence record is disgust. The only thing that is worse is being a sexual predator.

Listen, in this world today, there are no secrets. There is always someone, somewhere, who can find out anything about you. Imagine, for example, attempting to apply for as new job, and your prospective employer does a background check on you. If that domestic violence charge appears, you now become, in your prospective employers' eyes, that Neanderthal or punk or batterer that you were reading about several pages ago. It is far easier for the prospective employer to toss your resume and consider Mr. Clean on the next resume. Even if your would-be employer were to call you back – this is a real long shot – you will have to be able to come up with hell of an explanation in one hell of a short period of time, just to pull even with Mr. Clean and his peers, who are also vying for employment. And even if, by some miracle (they really needed people) you get this job, you will be seen by some as short tempered, unstable, and a potential problem employee, especially if some of those in the position to know are women.

Realistically, you will probably never get that chance to explain.

Well, you might ask. What about your ex? In this example, the courts, for once, were fair, and they gave her the very same domestic violence charge as they did you. And hey, she is looking for the exact same job as you are. She is competitive like that. But, in marked contrast to what the prospective employer thought of you, they more than likely will treat her as a victim. They might even become curious, (especially with a female boss) and they might ask her, ever so gently, "What happened, dear?" And, all she has to say is "I fought back". With that, she is in the clear, right next to Ms. Clean. Your ex might even be perceived as a fighter, one who is able to overcome adversity, and a problem solver (she called the police, right?). All of that, with just three words. She would probably get the job, and you will still have to pay alimony.

By now, you should get the point.

At least, you'd better.

Another Alternative

There is another, alternative way to deal with a failing, volatile relationship and/or the potential for domestic violence. This is almost a sure-fire way of making yourself nearly immune form the potential losses and setbacks of a domestic violence conviction. The only thing is, doing this task requires a huge amount of mental effort. So, what is this magic elixir that could be a potential lifesaver?

Become emotionally uninvolved with your spouse.

Yes, I said it. At first, at least, pretend like you don't care about your spouse, and whatever she does. And then, you should move yourself, mentally and emotionally, to that point where you really don't care. Here, I am expanding on a plan of action that includes non-action, for dealing with your spouse.

Mister, your reaction might be, well, you're crazy. And my reply to you is well, these are crazy times. The singular goal of this book is to enlighten the American male about what is going on in American society, and to make him smarter in reacting to what goes on with the American woman. And, so here it is. Think of this as one big option. The penalties for being found guilty of domestic violence – or even being found guilty of bad sexual relations – are increasing, publicly, all of the time. Just think about that football player who, in 2014, was fired from his $40 million contract with an NFL football team. People in society – none named, mind you – repeatedly cast blame upon the NFL after a video was "discovered" that showed the football player punching out his wife in an Atlantic City casino elevator. The thing is, that by the time the video appeared, this case had already been adjudicated by the justice system in that county. So, why was the NFL and the football team for which he played for put under intense public pressure to discipline and sanction this man, which they did? Is it because of the underlying racial overtones ever present within the United States? Did the NFL fail to somehow keep this big, dangerous black man under control?

I don't really like to comment upon whatever is in the media at this moment. Five years from now, this will all be forgotten about. Something else will happen. But I need to mention this incident because I feel what has happened is that with this incident, there has been a shift in how much that a man should be punished with a domestic violence incident. It seems that the justice system is no longer enough to satisfy the American woman's collective judgment against men who do wrong. It seems that this man must now be punished by going after his livelihood. He must be punished by going after who he is to himself.

At this point, I must ask, is this relationship worth it? It must be, to him, because he married her. It must be, to her, because she married him. Maybe she is one of those women who want to know "where the lines are", meaning, that she will test her man to see how much he tolerates. Who knows. As of this writing, this case is not decided within the NFL. But suppose everything goes downhill? Suppose the man loses everything, the $40 million contract, everything. Will she still want to be married to him, when he gets his new job as a taxicab driver? Will she be happy when they sit down to share their new evening meal, their individual cans of tuna fish? Will they fight over who gets to use the can opener first? And, here is the number one question. Was she worth $40 million?

You might ask, what does that case have to do with you asking me to become emotionally uninvolved with my spouse or girlfriend?

My answer is, everything. Just imagine what would have been saved, for that man personally, and men in general, if he didn't hit her, even if he was under the greatest provocation.

Now, to get you to see what I am proposing here, I need you, the male, to imagine what would you do, if you were that football player. Or, you don't have to be that football player. What would you do if you had a high paying, high profile job? And now your relationship has turned volatile? Now, the thought of becoming emotionally uninvolved may not be such a bad idea after all, no?

But, do we need a high profile job in order to consider this? I don't think so. But consider this other, even stronger fact as well. The whole domestic violence machinery depends upon your actions. Normally, (can't say 100%) she can't call the police unless you hit or holler at her. The courts can't sanction you until you have been thrown into the justice system by the police. Remember, it always takes two. A woman can't be a victim by herself. Listen, if your relationship has gone off the rails, you need to avoid public confrontation. And if you begin to emotionally distance yourself, and fall out of love, you could be saving yourself from a possible embarrassing and career ending incident of domestic violence. Even if you are that cab driver.

Now, most women do not like being ignored. They do not like their men trying to be emotionally distant from them. After all, every woman knows that their influence, and manipulations works best when you, the man is emotionally involved. They might engineer further confrontations. They might flirt with other men. They might have sex with other men, just to get you involved in a domestic violence incident. It will be up to you to hold on to your last nerve and think ahead and not go down that road with them.

In divorce court, your spouse might say that you have become emotionally distant, and so you abandoned her. This resonates more, of course, with female judges. You can counter by saying that she is unstable, and that you were trying to prevent a domestic violence incident without having to move from your shared domicile. Eventually, you will get over your pain and heartbreak, long before the consequences of a domestic violence conviction fade away.

MISCELLANEOUS

Miscellaneous

In this chapter I will try and cover some of the many other facets of our favorite subject that does not quite belong with the previous chapters. But there are still some other things that the American man needs to know. Some of the material that follows is highly subjective and might even border on the outrageous for some, but it still needs to be said. Trust me, women, as a group, know some outrageous things about you. Some of the things that they say are wrong (such as men cannot perform after age 53) but that does not stop them from being secure in their false knowledge about you. Furthermore, most women have easy access to a book or publication, or even a group of their peers, to discuss unusual things about men. As for men, I am not presently aware of any other book or publication that might "go there" when it comes to elevating the amount of knowledge for men.

In this chapter I will also try and take a look at what is happening in the near future for men and women in America. Some of the trends that are going on are a cause for concern. It seems to me that the washrag of victimization is being twisted once again. If you look at some of the things that are going on with women in the rest of the world, one begins to wonder just what is so bad within the United States.

For the Male College Student

Originally, I had targeted this book for the man who has gone beyond his normal college years but has not yet started a family. But some fairly recent items that had made the news in 2014 have made me reconsider, and add this one essay that is devoted to the young man of college age.

Young man, you need to be aware of the fact that when you go to college – even if it is in your own hometown – this is a transition from your life that was lived mostly at home to a life that will expose you to others whose values might be different from your own. Indeed, their values might be diametrically opposed to your own values. Furthermore, you may be exposed to others who may be far behind you – or far ahead of you – in terms of maturity and development.

And in the paragraph above, hell, I was just talking about the males that will soon be your peers. As far as the females go, you will need to apply perhaps five times the caution and forbearance that you used to apply to the neighborhood girls. After all, the young women that you may encounter may also have values that may be diametrically opposed to your own. And, you may meet young women who may be far behind you – or, more likely, far ahead of you – in terms of maturity and development.

And as often as not, a young woman of college age might still be on the road to discovering who she really is, as a sexual being. And that kind of slow development is something that you, the male, should be going through as well. This time should still be a time of mutual awareness raising for the both of you.

But, aside from all of that, young man, you really, really need to be aware of the changes that are now taking place in this society, as far as today's young women are concerned. You need to be aware because these changes are taking place mostly upon the nation's college campuses. There seems to be a new bow wave of the American woman's victimhood consciousness. For example, there seems to be a move afoot to expand the definition of rape from a forced sexual act to include "sex that I agreed to have but later I did not like". There is one Columbia University student who sees fit to carry around a (lightweight) mattress around with her, from class to class, because she is protesting her "rape". The young man who she had accused of this crime has been found innocent of raping her, months ago. The two had conventional sex and then they tried anal sex. The young woman did not like the verdict and so she continues to protest, at least in 2014. Perhaps what this young woman is really protesting is her failure of not having this man convicted. Another emerging body of thought is that there is an epidemic of sexual assaults against women taking place upon the nation's college campuses. Women's advocates contend that as much as 20 percent of all college age women have suffered a sexual assault. But a recently released report by the Justice Department's Bureau of Justice Statistics' National Crime Survey says that the rate of student sexual assaults is actually not 20 percent but 6.1 percent, per 1,000 women. And this is actually lower than the rate for those women who are not students – that rate is 7.6 percent per 1,000 women. Aside from the feminist motivations of pumping up the danger for women (men, of course, are on their own) how, then, does one define sexual assault? A cursory search online found these three examples. Sexual assault is defined as:

"Any involuntary sexual act in which a person is coerced or physically forced to engage in…." (Wikipedia)

"Assault of a sexual nature against another person" (USlegal)

"An individual engages in sexual activity without the explicit consent of the other individual involved." (Sarah Lawrence College)

And here is the definition of the word "assault" just in case you did not know.

"The act of creating apprehension of an imminent harmful or offensive contact with a person"(Wikipedia)

"A criminal act involving both a threat of violence and actual physical contact with the victim" (Yahoo)

Apparently, you do not even have to touch another person to be accused of assault, as far as Wikipedia is concerned. Personally I always thought that the act of hitting someone is an assault. But getting back to the earlier definitions of sexual assault, you can see that all three of the sexual assault definitions strive to be gender neutral. But, we all know that when it comes to initiating sex, the male is almost always proactive, and the female is almost always passive. In my opinion, the Wikipedia definition (".....in which a person is coerced or forced to engage...") is pretty close to rape. The USlegal version seems to cast a "wider net" and can seem to get you into trouble faster. With the "...assault of a sexual nature on another person..." it could be construed that a kiss on the cheek, or even a promised kiss on the cheek, could be construed as a sexual assault. But the third definition is the one that concerns me the most. The Sarah Lawrence College definition is the one that takes a sharply feminist slant with "an individual engages in sexual activity without the explicit consent of the other individual involved".

But most girls or women, during a kissing session or even heavy petting, will not tell you, the male, outright what they want you to do to them, or how far they want you to go. Most women have a predetermined idea of how far it should go, but this may change, according to how well you kiss and hold them. Most of the time, the female will simply wait on you to make the move, and then they will decide for themselves whether that move you just made feels alright to them. If so, they will just simply permit it to happen. Nothing destroys these moments more than saying "Do I have permission to remove your blouse? Or your bra?" Or, "Are we going to have sex?"

Now, let me say this, young man. If you perceive any hesitation or resistance from her at all, you should end the sexual encounter right away. If she decides later that she did not like the sex that she had, and now plans to get you arrested for sexual assault or worse, (especially at Sarah Lawrence College), she can simply deny that any questioning took place.

Furthermore, New York State (of course) recently enacted the Women's Equality Act. One feature of this raft of laws is that a woman's (but not a man's, how is that equal) use of drugs or alcohol not be considered as a factor when a female student has reported that she has been sexually assaulted. This is why I say "Don't touch a drunk female student, ever!", in my advertising for this book. This includes trying to help her back to her dorm room. If she reports a sexual assault or rape on the next day, all of her friends, and all of your former friends, will report that you were the last one with her. Now, your parents are on the hook for $20,000 in legal fees for your defense, even if you don't spend the next semester in jail.

Recently, this deadly (to your academic life) "Gotcha" game has gone beyond just sex. Some of the things that you say, even if it is directed to other men, can be cause for sanction if a female student hears it and decides that she does not like it. Please, please research some recent United States Department of Justice letters to the Universities of New Mexico and Montana. Also, take a long look at the Title IV and Title IX legislation for women (they need no further introduction).

The Rise of the Entitled American Bitch

Yes, the title might be a little incendiary, but so are some of the things that are happening around the country. There is a vocal minority (so far) of American women who are playing, or seem to be playing, that victim card over and over again, in widely publicized news stories. Sometimes, a woman even places herself in a position to be "victimized", like the woman who walked 25 miles over ten hours within the streets of Manhattan. She collected over 100 catcalls and compliments from male passers-by. Apparently, the goal of all this is to portray herself as a victim, and to portray all men as oafs and louts. Perhaps this woman was trying to show that the daily routine of women walking in the city streets is actually a tightrope walk of intimidation and danger.

This is, to me, a case of a woman who is playing the victimhood of woman for profit and a little fame. And never mind the fact that those men were not disrespectful to her. I do not know this woman, but you cannot tell me that she has never dressed provocatively to encourage comment by men, or that she has never enjoyed a favor done for her by a man. I also wonder how she ever met the man who accompanied her on this walk. He walked ahead of her with a video camera strapped to the back of his head or shoulders or whatever. This man must have, somehow, found a way to communicate to this woman something that she actually liked to hear – that day. I wish only that this woman, and others who think like her, would wear some kind of tee shirt or locket or cap or whatever else that would tell the prospective male that any comment would not be appreciated.

Again, I would like to point out that a woman's "actions" when it comes to interactions with men, are mostly passive. A man, almost by definition, has to be proactive if something is going to happen. Yet, it seems to me that some women are no longer interested in simply understanding that some men are simply trying to reach out to them. And these same women won't say or do anything to take themselves out of contention as well. I have yet to see a tee shirt or whatever that says "Don't talk to me". Instead, there is a "new standard" in that only the man that a particular woman approves of, has permission to speak out to her. All other men, in her opinion, are potential victimizers and rapists.

The thing is, how in hell are we men supposed to know, at a glance, which woman has "pre-approved" us? Apparently, the answer is not to ever say anything to a woman on the street, even if she is naked, because this is the new harassment. Perhaps the only approved ways for a man to meet a woman now is online, or at a party. But the party introductions might also become "verboten", because, after all the man has to start the conversation.

It helps, I guess if you, the man, are well dressed or rich and famous (what if a famous actor, like maybe George Clooney, spoke to the comment collecting woman? Would she abandon her experiment and the boyfriend, and jump into the actor's waiting limousine?) or better yet, even infamous, like the 80 something year old serial killer Charles Mansion, who attracted the attention of a 26 year old female fan, who wanted to marry him. There is a difference between being famous and infamous, but people don't much care anymore. I suspect that the main attraction is having money, or the appearance of having money (most women can't tell the difference). And having a lot of money entitles the man to anything he wants, if we are to believe all of the women who are flocking to the movie "Fifty Shades of Grey".

Now, let us take another turn on the American woman's hypocrisy wheel, and say what do you know? You have actually met one of those women who cannot stand to hear men who comment to them on the street. After a while, you might even get to know her. Well, guess what? All that they want from you is <u>manhood</u>. The old fashioned kind of manhood. They want you to take them out, order their meals for them, and then pay for it all, of course. They want you to be romantic, and use some of the same words that would have gotten you into trouble had you used them on the street, as a stranger. You must notice and compliment them without a hint each time that you see them. They want you to take the lead while dancing and during sex. Both acts must be flawless. They want you to direct the sexual episode and be responsible for their orgasm. You should be able to know what to do without them telling you. She may want you to pull her hair during sex, but only upon her non-verbal cue. When the two of you are again out in the street, she must feel protected, and you must defend her, verbally and physically. You must become violent on her demand. You must also return to passivity almost instantly.

Just don't say anything to her on the street.

And then there is the new wave of women's victimhood on the college campuses, which was discussed earlier. Another goal of this publicizing of victimization is to force the government to pass ever more restricting laws upon the things that men are likely to do. What this also does for women is to increase their personal power over men by having the state sanction and criminalize the behaviors of men. Perhaps within a couple of years, it will be unlawful to say anything to a woman you do not know on the street.

Now, let's finish this ride on the American woman's hypocrisy wheel, and let us take a look at what happens to women in other places on the planet. Whereas in the United States, where most American men are dismissed and denigrated as louts and socially inept, a cursory look at other parts of the world reveals a far harder life for some women at the hands of men elsewhere.

In countries such as India and Pakistan, where arraigned marriages are commonplace, most of these types of marriages are successful. But when things go bad here, they go very bad, when the would be bride does not like the groom and his family. This may start off a rift between the two families. The groom's family often feels disrespected, and the dispute can end in what is known as an honor killing. The would be bride is sometimes murdered, or more often, disfigured, just because she did not want the groom. And while it is usually a man who carries out these atrocities, the complicity of some of the women within the groom's family, such as the prospective mother in law, cannot be ruled out. Another type of honor killing can happen when it is discovered that a woman - usually a wife, or someone's girlfriend - was raped. Even though everyone around this woman has the ability to understand - if they want to - that this woman was the victim - yes, she was the victim - of this crime, the overwhelming thought is that she has brought down shame upon her entire family because she was the unwilling victim of rape. It is hard for someone from the West - especially the United States - to understand, but this is what happens. There have even been honor killings of both types within some immigrant communities within the United States. The relative silence of the immigrant woman, even within the U.S, where they can speak out freely, has been deafening. The same can be said for the silence of the American woman on this subject.

In 2014, the Islamic terrorist/expansionist group Islamic State has performed grisly single and mass executions in several Middle Eastern countries where they have taken territory. Some of these executions have been put online. The group has invaded and torn apart a local tribe in Syria by killing off the men and "distributing" the dead men's wives to their own soldiers for rape and ownership. The children of the tribal families were partitioned out, as well. Young boys were "enlisted" by the fighters to carry arms and bombs. Young girls were sold off as house slaves, or even worse, to pederasts. these types of crimes are not new, and not just carried out by Muslims, or those criminals hiding behind religion. During the violent breakup of Yugoslavia in the 1990's, Muslim women who were captured were raped en masse - until the majority of these women got pregnant. They then were imprisoned until they gave birth to the rapist's children. It was the soldiers fighting for independence within that country who were the rapists and kidnappers.

Now, I'm not saying that the American woman should be fired by anger, get up, and run over to Syria, and fight. But there are plenty of well off American women who could try and reach out, and maybe set up a charity or some other kind of help for these Syrian women.

An Iranian women has received a sentence of a year in jail, simply for attending a soccer match reserved exclusively for men. Yet, there is no one accusing Iranian men of being louts or predators.

The one incident that did inspire some American women to get up and protest was the kidnapping of a couple hundred Nigerian girls from a boarding school in that country. However, the will and the fighting resistance of a group called the Boko Hiram has outlasted the international outrage. The group has since moved on to even greater atrocities, such as killing off an entire village, and burning people alive within a locked up building. But, the Western world (both the American man and woman, this time) have now set their sights elsewhere.

In the rest of the world, the rights and freedoms of women vary, between the full rights and freedoms accorded women in northern Europe, and then the U.S., to the very limited rights accorded those women in the Middle East, and parts of Africa. Against this world background then, we see the American woman, sitting back and watching all this on TV in (relative) luxury. Yet, some American women still find time to fault and complain about the American man. One must wonder, then, if these women have turned into a Entitled American Bitch.

Is it all Prostitution?

There I go again, with the provocative title. But the word "prostitution" has lost most of its usage in just the past couple of years. As far as women's advocates and most law enforcement are concerned, "prostitution" is a word that too many people have become used to. "Human Trafficking" is the new byword nowadays, because the words invoke images of slavery style horrors and beatings of defenseless woman. While this type of crime certainly does exist, the American feminist has pumped it up big time. Every woman who sells herself on the street is a victim of human trafficking, and every man who buys that woman is automatically a supporter of human trafficking. The American man has largely bought, and swallowed this shit whole, without a whimper of protest. With all of this trafficking and victimization of women going on, it is a wonder how European countries have managed and allow prostitution to be legal and take place over there. Don't their women feel victimized?

Funny thing is, even with all of this official ban against "trafficking" and the decidedly negative stamp and criminal record against those who "supported" that crime, is that the American man is always paying for the American woman anyway. The reality, and message, from the American feminist society to the American man is that paying for an orgasm, which is what the man really wants, is "bad", and must be criminalized. However, paying for the American woman's time spent with you, is "good" and so this is encouraged. On the face of it, men have to spend money on women, from the first date until the final divorce, and even after that. This has not changed, even after a couple of generations after the women's movement. Furthermore, the American woman, through her liberation, has successfully managed to pick and choose exactly which parts of her liberation emancipates and benefits them, and which parts of the old lifestyle that they wish to keep. How many working women, after they get married, wish to stop working and become a stay at home wife? How many actually do this? In any case, these trends will stay this way because most men have not seen fit to question this.

But the times, they are slowly changing. It is projected that the current class of millennial students graduating from college will feature females, as a group, earning more money than males for the first time. And, there have been more female college graduates than males for quite some time. And, there have been more American females in the work force than males, since the recession of 2009. Now, do you think that the current female attitudes about men paying will change? The younger generation of men do not seem to be embarrassed by asking a woman for money. Perhaps the young women of today don't mind supporting a man. Or, are women slowly painting themselves into a corner, with so many of them having to compete for fewer and fewer men who are "marriageable?" (Translation... men who make more money).

So now, we can look to that body of divorce and family law that has, up until now, protected the American woman, no matter what lifestyle that she chooses. Will men, as the new "junior partner" within the marriage benefit? Some already have. But it is unlikely that there will be an "equalization" of men who will benefit from divorce in the future just the way that women do today. It will be interesting to watch how the individual states will rush – or not rush – to protect the status of women after a divorce. Some states, like New York (again, of course) are already prepared for this eventuality. See the "Look at the divorce laws" essay.

I look back, sometimes in amazement, just how the American woman's movement has left man in pretty much the same place as they were two generations ago. I also think that this is the crux of the problem. You cannot liberate one half of society and keep the other half in the same place as before. This creates a gap between the two groups. This is a gap of perception that, for some, becomes a bitter reality. This is a gap that is partially responsible for this book.

Become A Sex Tourist!

Yeah, I said it. I said "become a sex tourist". But, before you jump into yet another set of prejudgments, let me explain exactly what I mean by "sex tourists".

My definition of being a sex tourist is a person who has, or who will travel to another country for the purpose to interact with, and maybe have sex with women who live in these other countries. And that is the only definition that I am using. When I suggest to you, the American man, that you should go beyond our borders to meet women, I DO NOT mean having sex with underage girls, or sex trafficking, or any of the other bullshit that has been attached to the term "sex tourist" in recent times by feminists and lawmakers, both female and male, in yet another attempt to corral and make wrong the things that men are likely to do. Ironically, American women are some of the biggest sex tourists in the world, although you'll never hear them say that. Yeah, sure, your girlfriend went to Italy, just for those pair of shoes, and of course she did not want to get hit on by Italian men.

Listen, I have done this, mostly in Europe. And I have discovered, quite by accident, that women in other countries are not engaged in the not so quiet battle of the sexes as they are here in the good 'ol USA. You don't even have to have sex with those women to find this out. (That means you married men can also go and see for yourself). You don't even have to go as far as Europe to see the difference. Canada and Mexico are fine examples of how women and men get along, or at least interact, at a higher level than in the States. Men are treated like men elsewhere in the world. Men are not the bothersome perverts like they are made out to be like here in the good 'ol USA. Men are not used for their wallets to the extent that it happens in the USA. That doesn't mean, American man, that you are entitled to act out just because you're in another country. What I mean is, that if you go over there, meet someone, and treat her with respect (try learning a little of the language), chances are that you'll have a better time (even if it's only a conversation) than with an American woman.

Having said that, let me add the following caveats. You're not just going to go anywhere and do this. Saudi Arabia, for example, is out of the question. You cannot be a tourist there, for any reason, unless you are Muslim and are going to Mecca. In much of the Muslim world, as well as counties such as Pakistan and even India, to a certain extent, men and women are often separated, and starting conversations in the street is bad manners, to say the least. Iran, and even Russia, are out, of course, for current geopolitical reasons. Touching a woman in South Korea can spark a fight – with other men. Do your research. Don't get caught spending 20 years behind bars, just for crossing the borders, or trying to say how pretty she is. Don't make the United States spend $50 million for a marine raid to get your ass out of there. And one more thing. Keep your mouth shut, and bring home a pair of shoes.

Have you ever noticed that prostitution is legal in much of the world, but of course, not so much so in the United States? Yes, prostitution is legal in Nevada, but that "industry" is tightly controlled by a select few insiders. What the women charge there is often way out of reach for the middle class man. They charge a price that may be equal to the cost of a six month relationship with a "regular" woman. It's really male exploitation, and one does not have to be a patron to find this out. There were some reality cable TV shows that covered these houses of prostitution. And while "illegal" prostitution is everywhere, in the USA it is not worth it anywhere. In New York City, for example, the authorities will confiscate your car if you have used it to solicit a prostitute. And most strip clubs are a rip off as well. There are places close to the United States where you can discreetly indulge yourself.

On the other hand, New York, like every other state in the union, will <u>enforce</u> prostitution as long as we call it by another name. Think about this – your soon to be ex-wife has told the judge that she has cooked and cleaned for you and therefore, she must get paid. And so, we call this alimony, or maintenance. Legally, she must enjoy the same lifestyle that you gave her. You, the male, do not have this guarantee. Actually, we can call this pimping, because she is receiving money based on your labor and doing nothing for it. And, yes, the terms I've used fit, and I don't give a shit what anybody says about it.

And let's look at another facet of prostitution. Here in the good 'ol USA, where prostitution is mostly banned, quite a few American women have some form of mental baggage with them, ranging from entitlement to bitch potential. In many other countries, prostitution is at least tolerated, and yet the women in these countries have little or no anti-male baggage; they treat their fellow man like a fellow human being. Is there a correlation between the two? Are women "nicer" over there because they have to be? Are women nicer over there because men have a choice? Actually, I don't think so. It's just a part of the culture in many other countries that men and women still tend toward treating one another with respect. And yes, I know that there are many women right here within the USA that will treat you with respect. But to me, they always seem to be on guard, ever ready for the wrong word or gesture.

Let me give you an example of what I am talking about. I was once at the Second Avenue station in the New York City subway, in lower Manhattan.

At the time, the V train was running, and so one of those trains was idling in the station. A woman entered the nearly empty subway car. She was barely dressed, even allowing for the warm summer day up above. She wore sunglasses, a white blouse opened to partially reveal her ample chest above and tied up tight to reveal her belly button below, and on a flat stomach, I might add. She wore tight blue jean shorts which were just long enough to cover her butt cheeks. She had long legs with the fit body to match; and she was above average from what you see even in lower Manhattan. She found a seat and then sat down. A few minutes later a tourist came along. The guy was Brazilian; that country's flag was on a gold chain that he had around his neck. On his shoulder, he had his camera. Once he saw that woman, he said wow! to himself and he came into the car. He complimented the woman, and asked if he might take a picture of her.

Well, to the surprise of both of us, that woman verbally blew up in that man's face. She called him a bastard, and don't you dare take a picture of me, and you're nothing more than a pervert, and a few other cuss words. The man left the subway car totally perplexed.

This probably would not have happened on a subway train in Sao Paulo or Rio de Janeiro.

How does your woman feel?

So, really, how does your wife or girlfriend feel? Don't bother asking her. I am asking you, the male. This is not about how she feels, or whether she has a headache or whatever. This is about how she feels, to you. Down there. Yes, we are going to go way over into the red zone of the TMI (too much information) meter. After all, we have gone over practically everything else, haven't we? So, yes, I'm going to discuss how your wife's or girlfriend's vagina feels to you. I am not being sensational or scatological; this information is as important to you, mister, as is the knowledge of your states' family and divorce laws.

Have you even thought about this, mister? Has it ever occurred to you that you should pay attention as to how her vagina feels to you, upon penetration? Okay, mister, let's take it from the top. Women, in case you did not notice, come in all shapes and sizes. The same thing is true for their vaginas. And, yes, you, the male, can often tell whether a woman has just used her vagina, or whether she uses it a lot, or not so much. For each sexual act, the vagina must dilate, or prepare for penetration. After each sexual penetration, the vagina will return to its normal state of being contracted or closed. It takes, depending upon how many times the woman has had sex, roughly from one to three hours for the vagina to return to its normal state of being contracted or closed. This is why, when two women are in a lesbian relationship, where one woman suspects the other of cheating, the suspicious woman will demand that the other woman partially remove her clothing so that she can digitally (with her fingers) check the other woman to see if she has been penetrated or sexually excited. Women know this fact about each other, and they aren't afraid to find out. Again, it takes about one two three hours for the vagina to return to normal.

If you think that your woman has been out cheating, don't be afraid to tell her that you will digitally check her out, if necessary, at the next time she comes in late or out of character. You must always tell her beforehand in order to avoid a fight over the subject. (However, you might still fight over the cheating). If she does not allow you to check her vagina digitally, then you have 3/4th of an answer to your suspicions. Ironically some women fell that they have the right to bend down and smell your crotch whenever you come home late.

Now, let's take a closer look at that word, "normal". Please allow me to narrow the definition of it. "Normal" is what I mean when you might look at your woman's vagina when she is taking a shower. Normal is when you look down there on her, and all you see is just a patch of pubic hair, if she has not shaved. When a woman has just recently had sex, of if she has had a lot of "traffic" down there, her vagina has not yet, or no longer returns all the way back to its normal state, you, the man, can now see her vaginal lips through that patch of hair. This is what you are feeling for when you check her digitally. Some women shave their vaginas just because of this reason. A man can still discern the state of her vagina by just looking at her a little longer. Unfortunately, if your girlfriend or wife is or was a whore or a prostitute it can be a lot harder to tell when she has had sex.

Now, let's go all the way around this TMI circle and let us talk about your subjective judgment. Yes, I mean your subjective judgment, and not mine, for once. How does your girlfriend or wife really feel, during normal (missionary position) sex? There should be roughly the same resistance to penetration, the same amount of natural vaginal lubrication or wetness, every time the two of you do that same sex act (like most other people). Her vagina should not really feel any different unless you have really, really teased her (doubtful – you're a man) – or she is on her period. If you have sex with her while she is on her period, the blood from her menstrual cycle feels sticky and you will notice its bright red tinge.

Now, let's go a lot further. When a woman cheats, she prefers to sleep with her lover first, and give the "sloppy seconds", to you, the husband or boyfriend. Listen gentlemen, it was a woman who told me that. This means that they hold the lover in a higher esteem than they have for you. Let me say that again. The lover has a higher value to her (at least sexually) than you have, in her eyes. After a woman has had her lover and has come home to you, her vagina is wet, but not in the usual way. A man's sperm is thicker than a woman's vaginal juices. When you insert yourself into a woman that has already had another man (within three hours), you will actually feel the presence of another man's sperm in her. A man's sperm that is already in her vagina will feel lumpy, and sometimes even cold, to you, the second man. If you have vigorous sex with her, the previous man's sperm will often be pumped out of her. A woman's vaginal juices never feels lumpy. A woman's vagina with male sperm in her often does feel lumpy. Trust me, I know about these things, from experience, when I was in the Army, and elsewhere.

Most women like to think that you can't tell the differences in their vaginas, but I just told you how to tell the difference. Most women like to think that they can outsmart a man, especially when it comes to cheating. However, they cannot outsmart the fact that they often must receive a man's sperm, and that they can't remove it unless the douche very thoroughly. But, for them, performing a douche removes much of the sexual thrill at having had two (or more) men in one day. Women like to think that they can get away with this, for weeks, or even months. For you, the man, her actions are not only the lowest forms of disrespect, but they are also an invitation to share a sexually transmitted disease. And a woman will almost always lie and never take responsibility for that.

What you, the man, should do, if you feel that your woman is cheating, and you experience an abnormally wet and lumpy vagina once, say nothing, but urinate right away after sex. Sometimes, the urine stream can wash away some foreign matter. Wash your penis as well, concentrating on the tip. Do not lay up inside of her. If this happens again, tell your woman that you will be more comfortable in using a condom in the future. Look closely at her face when you say this to her. If she does not have a lot to say about this within about 30 seconds, then she more than likely was cheating. Most women have a thick file of ready lies in their heads, ready to launch at a man. Few of them have a lie that can go against what you just told them. It is now time to take a look around the rest of your shared lives and see what other clues to cheating that she may have left. Depending on how deeply involved you were with her, you, the man, need to work on getting yourself out of that relationship.

In Closing

My hope is that you, mister – yes, you guys – when you finally put this book down, you'll put it down as a newly enlightened man. You'll put it down as someone who is aware of the changes that have been wrought in this false war of men and women within the American society. I hope that you will be able to make changes and improve the quality – not necessarily the quantity – of the females in your life. And if you go ahead and marry a quality woman, you will not have to worry about the dangers of divorce because you did your homework and the two of you are soulmates anyway. I know that word "soulmates" may be overused, but the word is apt for what your ultimate goal should be. And, by the way, in order to keep and hold this quality woman, well, you will have to be a quality man.

ABOUT THE AUTHOR

Torin Reid is a born and raised resident of New York City. He has learned a lot, and has researched a lot more, about life while trying to participate in the lives of his two grown sons. Mr. Reid was once a civil service worker within the city. He has written magazine articles about transportation for over twenty years before writing this, his first full length book.

Comments about this book are encouraged. These comments may be used in another, future book about men and women. Please use the email address of Bradley17Moore@gmail.com for your correspondence. Bradley More is the author's pen name. There is presently no other authorized email address for Torin Reid.

Printed in the United States
By Bookmasters